SHARK FRENZY

SHARK FRENZY

JOHN CLARK

Grosset & Dunlap • Publishers • New York

Library of Congress Catalog card number: 75-27094
ISBN 0-448-12032-1 (Trade Edition)
ISBN 0-448-13336-9 (Library Edition)
First printing
Printed in the United States of America

Pl. LI.

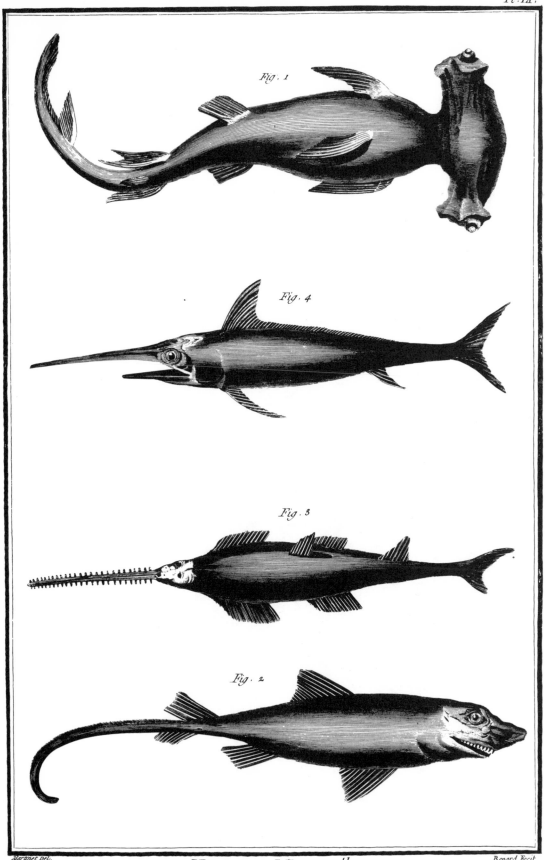

Fig. 1

Fig. 4

Fig. 3

Fig. 2

Martinet Del.

Benard Fecit

Histoire Naturelle,

Fig. 1. LE MARTEAU. Fig. 2. LE REQUIN. Fig. 3. LA SCIE. Fig. 4. L'ESPADON

FOREWORD

In science, we have a phrase that best describes this book: a "state-of-the-art report." It implies two things: one, that though information on the subject continues to grow, it is time to sum up what we know; and two, that there are elements of art in science. That is to say, while the collection of facts and the process of experimentation may be controlled by rigid rules, application of the findings to the affairs of mankind requires human judgment. In this report, I have reviewed the status of knowledge about shark attack, summarized and presented the salient facts, reached certain conclusions, and offered guidance to bathers and divers.

As a high order predator, the shark has survived through millions of years, not through brain power or intelligence, but rather through the evolution of senses of smell, vision and hearing finely tuned for ocean survival. While we cannot tune our senses to match those of the shark, we can use the finest evolutionary product of the human species, our reasoning ability. The more we know about sharks, the more we can apply that knowledge when we enter the ocean. As individuals we can avoid areas and times of high attack probability and prepare to defend ourselves in case we might be menaced by a shark. As communities we can take steps to make our beaches safer. The defense measures recommended in this book are feasible and all are rooted in basic scientific fact.

While the responsibility for the product is solely mine, I have benefited from the assistance of many colleagues. Particularly generous were H. David Baldridge and Perry W. Gilbert of the Mote Marine Laboratory; John G. Casey of the National Marine Fisheries Service; and Eugenie Clark of the University of Maryland. The Oceanographic Unit of the U.S. Coast Guard and particularly R. G. Cothren, provided exceptional help.

I wish to express my deepest gratitude to my research assistant, Catherine Lochner, the real stalwart of this project. Jeffrey Clark also assisted most ably, as did Phyllis Stein and Linda Clark.

ARK

A curious truce exists between shark and man, an arrangement that wavers uneasily between an accommodation to necessity and hostile fear. This state of affairs is permanent. It is no more possible for man to eradicate sharks from the sea than it is for sharks to eliminate man from the earth.

The vastness of the sea and its inhospitality make it totally impractical for us to mount a campaign of extermination. This same vastness and inhospitality, along with the state of helplessness it provokes, have fostered within us a primal fear of sea monsters and unpredictable and violent attack.

Each year about 50 documented shark attacks occur throughout the world, less than half of which are fatal. Added to the documented cases, there are undoubtedly many others that escape the official records. The major trouble spots are Australia, South Africa, and the United States. The U.S. attacks are concentrated in central California and along both coasts of Florida. The sharks that are most feared include the Great White, Tiger, Bull, Mako, Hammerhead, Sand Tiger and Whaler Sharks.

No matter that the statistical risk of death from shark attack is lower than that from a lightning strike or a bee sting. Such probabilities may comfort statisticians and apologists for sharks, but they do little to calm the fears of an aroused public. One thesis of this book is that while the risk of attack on any individual is miniscule, the anxiety this risk provokes may be immense. Another is that the correct way to deal with both the fear of sharks and the issue of protection is to provide useful information rather than mindless reassurance—information about the relation of shark to man, the character of particular sharks, the motives and tactics of shark attack, and the soundest methods of protection against sharks.

Sharks as Strangers

Since we live in such different environments, it is not surprising that the species of sharks are strangers to the races of man. Over the centuries we have invaded the shark world for reasons of commerce and recreation but have gained little familiarity with its inhabitants.

And sharks see so little of us that they have no need to familiarize themselves with our habits.

Moreover, man and shark often meet as enemies. Even the name "shark" reflects the evil reputation brought upon the tribe by misdeeds of a few of its species. The most accepted derivation of the word is the German root *Schurke,* meaning rogue, villain, rascal, sharper, scoundrel.

This enmity is shown in a letter of 1580 written by a traveler sailing on a vessel between Portugal and India, as reported in the journal *Fugger News-Letters* in 1580:

" . . . What called forth still greater surprise on my part were other big fishes that are in the ocean and that eat man alive, whereof I have been myself a witness. For when a man fell from our ship into the sea during a strong wind, so that we could not wait for him or come to his rescue in any other fashion, we threw out to him on a rope a wooden block especially prepared for that purpose. . . . But when our crew drew this block with the man toward the ship and had him within half the carrying distance of a musket shot, there appeared from below the surface of the sea a large monster called Tiburon; it rushed on the man and tore him to pieces before our very eyes. That surely was a grievous death. "

Sharks have always been the subject of myths. It might even be said that the mythological purpose was to explain the shark as a logical element of the natural world and assign to it a purpose. Thus to the Warrau Indians of South America, the constellation we know as Orion's Belt was the missing leg of Nohi-Abassi, cut off by a sister-in-law who disguised herself as a shark. This she did to wreak vengeance on him for arranging the murder of his mother-in-law by inducing a large shark to devour her.

On the Island of Hawaii, the Kapaaheo, or Shark-Stone, now in the Bishop Museum, derives its name not only from its sharklike appearance, but also from an ancient tale concerning the mysterious disappearance of maidens, one by one, as they swam in a sheltered cove. Whenever a maiden vanished, a stranger was seen near the cove. One day, fishermen armed with spears swam with the girls to protect them. When a shark attacked, the fishermen drove it off, stabbing it many times with their spears. Shortly afterward, the stranger was found on the beach dying of spear wounds. At death, his body turned into the Shark-Stone.

The sailor's life, always fertile with legend and superstition, has produced much shark lore. European sailors on slow square riggers, which were often followed by sharks, believed that catching a female shark, particularly if she was pregnant, portended a major event.

On the faster clipper ships it was traditional to nail the tail of a shark (or porpoise) to the bowsprit for good luck. In 1908, the bark *Avenir*, a training ship of the Belgian Navy, was preparing for its maiden voyage to the South Seas. Pointing out that the ship lacked the symbolic tail, many Scandinavian, Irish, and German sailors in the crew refused to sail.

In order to understand and deal with the dangers posed by sharks, primitive cultures often created a world view in which sharks had an important and understandable place. All coastal cultures seem to have deified the shark in some form or other. In Japanese legend, the shark was a terrifying figure—one storm god was known as Shark Man. Among the Polynesians, sharks were transformed into gods who were worshipped by the islanders. In the Solomon Islands, when certain men died, their souls entered the bodies of sharks, and these sharks were revered as guardian spirits or family gods. Each locality had its own set of shark gods, often based on a particular species of shark. In the Society Islands, for example, the Great Blue Shark was worshipped, while other shark species were killed and eaten. Altars were constructed to shark gods throughout the South Pacific, and sacrifices and rituals were performed to seek their favors. Each locality had beliefs and taboos associated with its particular sharks, and battles were fought when one group violated the shark taboos of another.

Once sharks were incorporated into a system of beliefs, and hence "understood," they could be controlled and manipulated for the benefit of the be-lievers. Thus, in the Solomons, "ancestor" sharks would not attack worshippers—but "wild" sharks, whose souls were not those of departed ancestors, would.

Properly invoked, sharks would bring good luck and protect their devotees during trips at sea and in other hazardous undertakings. On Samoa, the White Shark was an emissary of Moso, the land god. To guard his cocoanut or breadfruit tree from thieves, the Samoan would suspend an image of a shark from the tree. Any thief would run the risk of being bitten by a shark the next time he went fishing.

In Polynesia, more secular practices grew out of shark worship. In Hawaii, for example, a special shark corral of lava stone was built close to the "lair of the Queen Shark" at the edge of the harbor. Gladiators entered the corral to do battle with sharks enticed into it with both fish and human bait. The gladiator was armed with a shark-tooth spear—a short shaft with a single tooth attached. He waited until the shark charged, then tried to dive beneath it and rip its belly open with the spear—a rather one-sided battle.

These are some of the ways in which the leaders of coastal peoples incorporated the shark strangers into their cultures. Once they provided a reason for attack, they could use their people's primal fear of sharks to exercise control over them. Sharks have terrorized mariners over the centuries, and mariners have, in turn, exploited sharks. Sharks are still netted, hooked, and harpooned for their hides, fins, flesh, and oil. The hides of many species make excellent-quality leather when properly tanned. The Chinese penchant for soup of shark's fins is legendary, but it is less well known that the flesh of certain sharks is quite edible. Shark meat is converted by the Japanese to Kamaboko, a type of fishcake. Shark is often served in the fish-and-chips shops of England and Australia. Mako, Porbeagle, and other species are quite palatable, but, ironically, the favorite fare of the shark eater is the flesh of the Maneater or Great White Shark.

Sharks are much sought by small groups of avid sport fishers in New Zealand, Australia, South Africa, the United States, and Britain. The International Game Fish Association recognizes six species of shark as worthy quarry for anglers: the Mako, Porbeagle, Thresher, Tiger, Great White, and Blue Shark. Zane Grey once called the Mako "the aristocrat of all sharks." He elaborated: "It is really unfitting to call him a shark at all. . . . His leaps are prodigious, inconceivably high. The ease and grace . . . is indescribable."

The misfortunes of an inexperienced shark fisher are portrayed graphically by Sir Arthur Grimble in *A Pattern of Islands*. Failing to catch a shark with his sport tackle, Grimble arranged to put to sea in a native canoe, much to the amusement of the local villagers. A short distance from shore he put over a baited hook and waited for action:

> I was not yet settled back in my seat when the canoe took a shuddering leap backwards and my nose hit the foredeck. A roar went up from the crowd . . . the shark reversed direction. The back of my head cracked down on the deck behind me; my legs flew up. . . . In the next fifteen minutes, without one generous pause, that shark contrived to jerk, twist or bounce from my body for public exhibition every ignoble attitude of which a gangling frame, lost to all self-respect in a wild scrabble for handholds, is capable. The climax of its malice was in its last act. It floated belly up . . . as if quite dead. I piloted it into the shallows. There I tottered to my feet to deliver the coup-de-grace. But it flipped as the club swung down; I missed, hit the sea, somersaulted over its body, and stood on my head under water. . . . The beach was a sea of rolling brown bodies racked on the extremity of joy.

Sharks have starred in movies, inspired the plots of novels, and entertained millions of visitors to commercial aquariums throughout the world, where their size and ferocity make them a major attraction. During my stint as curator of the New York Aquarium, I found that Sand Tiger Sharks would coexist peaceably in tanks with live fish of many species providing that each day they were fed 2 pounds of dead fish per 100 pounds of body weight. The aquarium customers' favorite entertainment was watching the sharks consume their daily ration. But sharks can as easily cause frustration for their keepers.

David Davies in *About Sharks and Shark Attack* relates the sad story of Willie, a 6-foot Bull Shark (called a Zambesi Shark locally) caught for the Durban (South Africa) Aquarium in 1959. After a thirty-nine-day fast, Willie attacked and swallowed a 10-pound sting ray the moment it was deposited in her tank. She soon became the "boss" of the Aquarium population. Willie occasionally consumed her planned diet of dead fish, but more often "she preferred to make her own arrangements about meals." From September to December, she attacked and ate a large spotted beagle ray, various sting rays, duckbilled rays, skates, three much prized Dusky Sharks, and four or five Hound Sharks.

Members of the Ivan Tors film crew position a huge Tiger shark for a key scene in the James Bond film Thunderball.

Not only did Willie consume a toll of specimens in the tank, but following the seasonal increase in water temperature in December, she "appeared to be more than casually interested in the Aquarium divers who entered the tank regularly for routine cleaning operations." Obviously something had to be done to protect the divers.

By this time, however, Willie had become the favorite attraction in the Aquarium, and destroying her

Looking like a monster from a ghost story, this man-eating Tiger (top) is being "walked" around by a diver in a Marineland tank. When captured, sharks must be carefully tended until they regain their ability to swim.

Shark fishing has increased in popularity over the years, and tournaments are frequent. The spectacle of a catch of sharks will always attract a crowd. (National Marine Fisheries Service)

would not have been popular. On the other hand, the officials worried that every future Durban shark attack would be blamed on her if she were released into the open sea. They reluctantly decided on a swift disappearance as the best compromise. After two days of futile effort, she was finally hooked early on the third morning, lifted out of the tank, and hurriedly dispatched, sectioned, and whisked away with the trash before any visitors arrived. But a reporter did come within half an hour after the Aquarium opened to investigate the missing exhibit. The curator told him that during a "postmortem," a lobe of Willie's liver was found to be discolored. Thus Willie's sudden demise was attributed by the local newspaper to a "liver complaint"—not to her fearful eating habits.

Sharks are increasingly caught for use in experiments on many problems in human physiology, immunology, and virology, according to shark expert Perry W. Gilbert. They have thus become significant contributors to our knowledge of kidney physiology, osmoregulation, metabolism, cell metabolism, cancer, and antibody formation.

There is ample evidence that concentrated fishing does reduce the local populations of many dangerous species of sharks. Many U.S. experts believe that if commercial fishing for sharks in Florida could be made more profitable or sport fishing more popular, the abundance of sharks could be lowered and the risk of attack reduced. U.S. sport and commercial fishermen now catch a few hundred thousand sharks a year, but the effort is dictated by maximum pleasure or profit and not directed toward dangerous species or hazardous bathing beaches.

Sharks in Perspective

Sharks are a primitive tribe of creatures that have evolutionary roots in the Devonian period some 350 million years ago. Thus they have been on earth nearly one hundred times longer than man.

Sharks completely dominated the world ocean until perhaps 100 million years ago. Since then, their dominance has subsided and they now share the ocean with 20,000 species of "true" fishes. Still, the 250 species of sharks living today exert a strong influence on life in the ocean because they prey aggressively on so many other creatures that they serve to keep their populations in check.

Sharks are among the easiest of fishes to recognize as a group and among the most difficult to separate by species. The ones that are hammerheaded, long-tailed, gigantic, or brightly patterned are easy enough to classify, but these number only a few out of the 250 species. The rest show only small variations from the standard fin and body form. Most are slender and torpedo-shaped, tapering from the shoulders sharply forward to a pointed snout, and then more gradually rearward to a narrow tail stalk. The tail itself is broad and stiff, unlike that of a regular fish. The mouth is uniquely underslung. The forward, or pectoral, fins are very long and stiff, and the gills are vented through a series of five to seven parallel slits above the pectorals.

Sharks are most commonly colored in shades of gray, brown, or black on their backs, and white, buff, cream, or light gray on their bellies. This color system—a gradual shading from dark on the upper surface to light across the belly—is a camouflage pattern. A shark thus countershaded appears dark against a dark background when seen from above, and light against a light background when seen from below. A secondary effect of the color system is to distort dimension, causing the fish to look flat rather than solid, because the countershading balances the reflectivity of light coming from various directions. The total effect is an overall neutral tone, with no distinct break between upper and lower surfaces. In this way, a shark can be inconspicuous from any angle of view.

Usually some external feature or combination of features or shapes distinguishes a species. Occasion-

Dr. Perry Gilbert, one of the world's foremost ichthyologists, examines the eye of an anaesthetized Mako shark at Bimini in the Bahamas.

17

ally two species are so similar that comparative measurement of fins or examination of jaws or tooth structure is required. Detailed knowledge of tooth and jaw form is particularly useful in determining the species involved in an attack when a tooth has been left behind in the victim's body or when the imprint of the jaw on the victim is distinct enough for recognition.

Sharks have an unusual arrangement of teeth. In both upper and lower jaws, the front row of teeth is backed up by several rows of duplicate teeth. As a forward tooth is shed or broken away, another moves up from behind to replace it. For example, young Lemon Sharks automatically shed and replace their front teeth every eight to ten days. Each species has one, sometimes two, of the following general types of teeth: (1) thin triangular cutting teeth with very sharp edges; (2) long awl-shaped piercing teeth with sharp points; (3) flat molarlike crushing teeth. The teeth of any particular shark are sufficiently distinct in form to distinguish the species from all others.

Shark jaws are powerful. In laboratory tests, a typical 8-foot shark generated a pressure of 15 tons per square inch at its teeth tips. In action, as the shark approaches a large prey, it first raises its head and stabs the sharply pointed teeth of its lower jaw up into the flesh. The upper jaw, which is free of the skull, is then

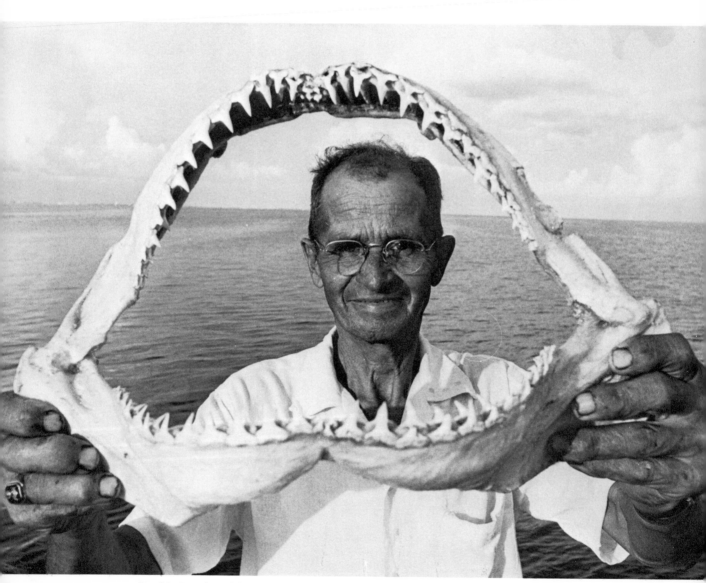

Freddy Friedewald displays tooth-studded jawbone of one of the many sharks he has hauled in over a decade of shark fishing.

protruded. The cutting teeth sink into the prey, and the shark then shakes its head violently from side to side until a large chunk is bitten off. If the prey is small enough, a shark will swallow it whole.

The underslung position of the shark's mouth has given rise to the popular fallacy that a shark must turn on its side or back in order to bite. Sharks may turn partly on their sides to reach prey on the surface, but they do not have to. A shark that opens its mouth and dashes forward to strike arrives mouth first. The front of him is all mouth, and he can bite a fish or a man from almost any position. The mouth of the White Shark and several other species is so far forward, and the jaws so protrusible, that the shark can bite floating objects easily without twisting on its sides. The White Shark can snap a full-grown porpoise or sea turtle in two with its jaws and teeth.

Shark skin is tougher than cowhide and its surface is protected by a latticework of scaly little barbed plates called dermal denticles, which are actually tiny teeth growing in the skin. Because of this, sharkskin is so extraordinarily abrasive that it can be used for sandpaper. The denticles must be removed in the process of tanning the hides to make leather.

The shark's unique skin contributes to the speed and the ease with which they swim. The denticles apparently provide a smooth or ''laminar'' flow of water along the sides of the shark, greatly reducing friction.

While sharks may cruise efficiently, they are severely limited in maneuverability. The fins are heavy and rigid and cannot be flexed like those of other fishes to hover, to back up, or to turn in tight spaces. Most sharks lunge straight ahead at their prey with jaws open and bite on the run. If a shark misses, it has to turn a complete circle and return for another lunge. For this reason sharks do not go after prey in confined places.

The large forward fins (pectorals) are shaped like airplane wings and serve primarily to aid the sharks in sustained swimming, adding upwards of 25 percent to their lift. This is a needed advantage because sharks do not have the internal buoyancy chamber, or swim bladder, typical of true fishes. They are heavy, and if they stop swimming, they will sink. The large oily liver (25 percent of the body weight of some sharks) provides some buoyancy, but sharks still weigh about 5 percent more than water.

Correlated with the shark's need to swim to remain afloat is its need to force water over the gills. While most fishes can pump water over their gills for respiration, sharks are without any pumping system and must swim constantly to force water over their gills. Consequently, sharks that are immobilized not only sink but suffocate.

Sharks' eyes shine in the dark like a cat's. A silvery layer behind the retina of the eye called the tapetum is responsible. Despite a general opinion that sharks have poor vision and are partially color-blind, they can see well enough and, like cats, have excellent vision at low light levels. Sharks are, in effect, creatures adapted to a nocturnal existence—or to life in the dimness of the ocean depths. Tests on Lemon Sharks show that sharks' eyes are so well adapted to darkness that the sensitivity of their eyes increases as much as one million times between daylight and darkness.

A real specialty of sharks is olfaction, the sense of smell. In fact, about two-thirds of the volume of the shark brain is composed of olfactory apparatus. Sharks are incredibly sensitive to smells and, like dogs, literally sniff their way about the world, sensing both prey and enemy by smells wafted on the tides and ocean currents. The nostrils, or nares, placed under the tip of the nose, allow water to pass efficiently over the olfactory sensors and out without going through the throat or mouth.

Sharks combine an extreme sensitivity to smell with a rapid and accurate directional ability and often a special zigzag swimming pattern. When a shark senses an odor, it begins a search pattern, zigging left when the odor is stronger in the left nostril, and zagging right when the odor is stronger in the right nostril. This rapidly leads the shark to the source of the odor. Blood in the water is particularly attractive to sharks, whether from fish or from man.

Sharks also have well-developed ''hearing.'' They are particularly keen at detecting distant sounds—sonic waves up to 640 cycles per second. However, the ears are placed so close together within the head that directional hearing is poor. To overcome this deficiency, sharks have a unique organ, the lateral line, which is a line of special sensors (neuromasts) buried just beneath the skin that extends from head to tail on both flanks. These sensors detect and pinpoint the exact direction of ''near-field'' sounds—strong vi-

Note the underslung mouth and curved back of this Black Tip shark as it lunges toward the bait.

*Shark undergoing the light sensitivity test,
which registers its range of vision and reaction to varying degrees of light.*

*Looking at the streamlined shape of this Lemon shark (left) as it cuts gracefully through the water,
one can easily understand why naval architects
have used the shark as a model for developing the submarine.*

brations from a localized source in the range of 10 to 200 cycles per second.

To learn how effective the shark auditory system is for locating prey, an Australian researcher, T. W. Brown, recorded on tape the sounds made by recently speared and violently struggling fish. He discovered that he could attract large and dangerous sharks of many species to any location by replaying the sounds through an underwater speaker.

Hearing is the shark's long-range sense, capable of detecting prey thousands of yards away. Smell appears to be most effective at hundreds of yards, although sharks can probably track strong odor trails for miles through the water. A sonic receptor called the lateral line comes into play at 100 feet or less. Vision becomes keen inside 50 feet, and at 10 feet or closer it is the primary sense.

The shark's sense of taste is strangely developed. Taste sensors are found not only in the mouth but over the outside of the snout as well. Sharks are often seen touching or pushing at objects with their snouts for the probable reason of testing a potential food object for palatability.

Unlike most true fishes that merely spawn their eggs into the water, sharks typically bear their young live. And since this requires a system of internal fertilization, the bellies of the males are equipped with a pair of special penislike copulatory organs called claspers. The claspers are erected as needed and used to insert semen into the paired genital openings of the female. The name ''claspers'' was given to the male organs by Aristotle, who erroneously concluded that the male used them to clasp the female during copulation.

While modern studies show that sharks do not use the claspers to gain dominance in courtship, males of the larger species have been observed bullying females into submission by persistent mild attacks with the jaws. This seems strange when one considers that the females of most shark species are heavier by 25 percent than the males and should easily be able to dominate them.

Aristotle's idea held at least through 1798, when the French naturalist, the Comte de Lacepède related the following charming account of shark reproduction in *Histoire Naturelle des Poissons:*

Barbels are the telltale trait of the Nurse shark. These enable the shark to taste the contents of the ocean floor as it searches for food.

" Held in this position by the hooked appendages of the male, by their mutual efforts, and by a kind of entwining of their many fins and the extremities of their tails, they float in this constrained position, but one which must to them be full of charm, until the life fluid of the male animates the eggs which have already reached a degree of development susceptible to receiving it. And such is the force of their active passion, which is aflame even in the midst of water, and whose heat penetrates even the most abysmal depths of the sea, that the male and female, which at other times would be so formidable to one another and would only seek to devour each other if they were pressed by violent hunger, are now softened and surrender to emotions quite different from those of destructiveness, mingling without fear their murderous weapons, bringing together their enormous jaws and terrible tails, and far from inflicting death, expose themselves to receive it rather than be separated, and not ceasing to defend with fury the object of their passionate enjoyment. "

Gestation time is one and one-half years or more. Litters range from two to a hundred ''pups,'' depending upon the species.

Most of the dangerous species of shark migrate vast distances during the course of each year's feeding and breeding cycle in order to find space and abundant nourishment. My colleague John Casey of the National Marine Fisheries Service, who has directed the marking of 13,000 sharks with identifying tags, finds that sharks cross the Atlantic, and some species migrate from the U.S. northeast coast to the Caribbean and South America. Data from the tags on recaught sharks show, for example, that a Thresher Shark traveled from North Carolina to Cuba, a Blue Shark from New York to Colombia, and a Mako from Rhode Island to Guyana.

Sharks grow very slowly but like all fishes, continue growing until death. A growth of 6 inches a year would be considered normal for many species. The most definitive data on growth is from sharks that were caught, measured, tagged, and then recaught and remeasured. One tagged when 3 feet long grew only 20 inches in the next seven years. The growth of another, tagged when 6 feet long, was too slight to be detected after seven years. It is therefore obvious that a large shark must be a very old shark.

Sharks are carnivorous, feeding on a wide variety of fishes, invertebrates, and other sharks. While some species are scavengers that indiscriminately consume all kinds of available food and refuse, the dangerous ones are restless and opportunistic predators, constantly on the prowl for victims. Shark expert Paul Budker explains this perfectly in *The Life of Sharks*:

The deadly underwater mating game of the Nurse shark. Courting begins with vicious biting of the female's soft underbelly. Unable to withstand the male's sustained attacks, she submits.

Men of the National Marine Fisheries Service tagging sharks. Tagging has provided scientists with valuable information on the migratory patterns of sharks.

> The ceaseless activity shown by sharks is consequent partly on their lack of a swim bladder . . . but partly also on their need to ensure for themselves a meal. . . . Their prey, often more swift or agile than they, flee at their approach, and the predator, to avoid death by starvation, must be in a constant state of readiness, living a life of perpetual ambush, pursuit and attack. In most fishes, however, and in sharks in particular, there is also the ability to fast for considerable periods.

The key to success for the shark is feeding efficiency—that is, the amount of food that can be assimilated by expending a given amount of energy. This input-output ratio governs growth, vigor, and the day-to-day survival of every shark alive.

Catching its food requires a large output of energy. There is a fine line between success and failure of attacks—big predators have to work hard for their daily meal, even in an area where forage is abundant. Sharks that are forced to spend more energy in feeding than they gain from the food they capture cannot keep up with their needs and eventually either die of starvation or are consumed by a predator in their weakened state.

In normal feeding, sharks consume in one week an amount of food ranging between 2 and 15 percent of their body weight. Older sharks tend to consume the lower percentage and young sharks the higher. However, their feeding habits are anything but predictable, and fishermen often find that sharks with full stomachs take bait as eagerly as those with empty ones.

A source of energy is necessary to assure fitness during times of enforced fasting—migration, low food availability, sickness, and the preoccupation of breeding. To this end, sharks are equipped with an especially large and efficient liver. It expands to accommodate great stores of oil during heavy feeding periods and reaches one-fifth or even one-quarter of the weight of the whole body. The shark can live off this store of oil for months, if necessary, without grave loss of energy and strength.

Some species hunt alone, others in packs. Some feed in strategic fashion, such as Thresher Sharks, which round up fish like aquatic cowboys, and Sand Tigers, which drive bait schools against a beach en masse. Others feed in more casual fashion. But none hunt for human prey—there are no systematic man-eaters.

Many sharks feed primarily on one or two species of prey, tracking them through the ocean on their seasonal wanderings. For example, Porbeagles specialize in mackerels, Sandbar Sharks in menhaden, and Mako in swordfish and bluefish.

Some sharks are prone to ingest strange objects. Examples include: a keg of nails, a chest containing pearls and precious stones, a bottle of fine Madeira wine, a car license plate, a chicken coop, a yellow-

Sharks often feed on smaller sharks, making a high mortality rate for baby sharks. Here, a Tiger devours a baby Lemon.

billed cuckoo. A privateer was once convicted by the British Navy on evidence recovered from a shark's stomach—incriminating papers thrown over the side during pursuit and later recovered by a shark fisherman aboard another vessel.

Many species of shark are prone to feeding frenzies when some bizarre feeding urge triggers them into an uncontrolled attack on anything in sight—tin cans, wooden boxes, other sharks, rafts. Triggered by human blood and vomit, such attacks have turned ship sinkings into massacres. Budker calls this "a sudden release of a kind of collective delirium of destruction."

Other than malefactors of its own tribe, a shark has little to fear from any creature in the sea except the killer whale, a species big enough, fast enough, and with jaws powerful enough to prey on sharks. Big sharks eat smaller sharks as a regular part of their diet. Another species that attacks sharks, but for reasons of territorial and personal defense, is the bottlenose dolphin, friend of man. Many sharks are fond of dolphin and eat them whenever they can catch them. The bottlenose retaliates, however, by ramming sharks in the gills, and a full-grown dolphin can easily dispatch a large shark in this fashion.

Among the natural friends of sharks are two types of fish: pilot fishes, which often escort sharks by the dozens in a sort of swimming retinue; and remoras, which ride free on shark bodies by attaching themselves to them with a vacuum disc that grows atop their heads. Both species probably benefit in this symbiotic partnership by picking up the leftovers from the shark's meals; how the shark benefits is yet unknown.

One or more of the many shark species can be found living almost everywhere in the world ocean. There are sharks that swim only in the high seas, sharks that inhabit only the darkest depths of the ocean and sharks that live out most of their lives near the coast, along the beaches or in the bays. Among these sharks that haunt the coastal shallows and are attackers, not more than a dozen species pose a serious threat. Each of them has its own special life style and each must be understood as a distinct and separate force operating

Large sharks, like this Lemon, are often accompanied by Remoras and other pilot fish that feed on scraps left over by the shark.

in the natural world. This world shall always hold mystery for us and its inhabitants shall always be something of strangers.

Sharks are found throughout most of the world ocean. Many species live and feed only at considerable depths, while others occupy the ocean surface layer or coastal shallows. It is the latter, which often cruise the surface with their dorsal fins breaking water, that most frequently come into contact with man. While most sharks are found in open waters, some do enter shallow coastal waters and even swim up rivers, particularly the Ganges River in India.

(Marineland of Florida)

YPES

Although they resemble each other in general form, the various shark species are as different from one another as cats are from bears. The smallest species, a freshwater variety, grows to only half a foot in length. The largest species reaches 50 feet in length and is the largest fish living in the sea.

Ichthyologists usually separate the sea fishes into two distinct categories: the sharks and rays, with cartilaginous skeletons, and the bony fishes, or true fishes, with calcified skeletons. In addition to basic bone structure, sharks are also distinguished from bony fishes by such anatomical differences as: five to seven gill slits instead of the single large gill flap of most bony fishes; a thick skin covered with toothlike plates called dermal denticles instead of fish-type scales; and an intestinal adaptation called the spiral valve that is unknown in the bony fishes.

Sharks belong to the taxonomic class of animals *Chondrichthyes,* and within it to the order *Pleurotremata.* The order is broken down into twenty separate families. Finally, sharks are categorized according to genus and species, the genus being a collection of similar species. Successful breeding takes place only at the species level; for example, a White Shark cannot breed with a Mako or any other shark species.

I have included in this chapter accounts of sharks that are prominent either because they are hazardous to man or because they possess some curious characteristic. The scientific designation (genus and species) is given in parentheses next to the common English name of each shark. A genus name followed by "spp" indicates that more than one species is included in the designation.

When most people think of sharks, they envision the large and vicious ones that threaten human life. Yet these number less than a dozen out of the hundreds of species of shark that live in the world ocean today. Dangerous sharks are found in the following four family groups: Sand Tiger Sharks (*Odontaspididae*), Hammerhead Sharks (*Sphyrnidae*), Mackerel Sharks (*Lamnidae*), and Requiem Sharks (*Carcharhinidae*).

The Sand Tiger family includes the Sand Tiger (U.S.), the Ragged Tooth (South Africa), and the Grey Nurse (Australia). The Hammerhead family includes all Hammerheads and Bonnetheads. The Mackerel Sharks include the White, Mako, and Porbeagle.

The Requiem Sharks include more than 100 species altogether, including five of the most dangerous of the maneaters. In addition to the notorious Tiger Shark, the family includes the Bull and Whaler Sharks, as well as the Lemon, Blacktip, and a dozen others that are known to have attacked man. The Requiem species are "typical-looking" sharks with large and sharp teeth that are generally triangular and platelike. The various species resemble one another so closely that usually it takes a trained ichthyologist to distinguish among them.

Great White Shark (carcharodon carcharias)

The White Shark has a worldwide reputation as the largest and most dangerous of the predatory sharks. Its nearest challenger in ferocity, the Tiger Shark, is smaller, threatens a lesser part of the ocean, and has claimed fewer human victims. Only the Whale Shark and the Basking Shark grow larger than the White, but they are mild-mannered cousins with tiny teeth that strain plankton and small fishes from the water for food.

The Great White Shark, as the species is formally known, is a member of a family, the *Lamnidae* or Mackerel Sharks, that also includes the Porbeagle and the Mako. Its scientific name gives double emphasis to the danger of its teeth: *Carcharodon* means "jagged tooth," and *carcharias* means "coarsely serrated teeth." In addition to "Maneater," a variety of synonymous common names are in use—Blue Pointer (Africa), White Pointer, and White Death (Australia).

White Sharks are dark blue, gray, or brown on their upper surface, fading to white or grayish white underneath. With age, the color gradually fades so that the larger ones often become a uniform leaden white or dun shade. The White Shark's fins are dark, nearly black at the tips, and there is a black spot at the "armpit" of the pectoral fin.

The body of the White Shark is superbly streamlined, with a finely tapered snout, a torpedo-shaped

*Great White savagely attacks forty-pound chunk of horsemeat
hung outside a protective cage during
Peter Benchley's shark expedition off Dangerous Reef, Australia.*

body, and a broad symmetrical tail. Slender when young, the shark becomes thick in the midsection as it grows older. From above, the head looks flat and wide. The pair of rearward lateral keels protruding from each side makes the shark appear to thicken just in front of its tail. The pectoral fins are long and sickle-shaped, the dorsal high and stout. The mouth is wide, set well back under the snout, and armed with fifty perfectly designed sharp thin teeth, teeth so deadly that their shape has become the symbol of man's fear of sharks.

Each tooth is a nearly exact triangle—flat, a bit higher than wide, and flaring a bit at the base. There is a heavy base but no root. The tooth is hollow and fragile. The edges are serrated (saw-edged) and exceedingly sharp. As is typical with sharks, the White Shark has several complete rows of teeth, one behind another, so that each frontal tooth is quickly replaced, if shed or broken, by a new one standing in the row just behind it. The largest teeth—3 inches in a 36-foot specimen—are in the front center of the jaw.

The White is a shark styled for speed. Powered by rapid beats of the strong tail, the body itself remains quite rigid while moving, strangely contrasting with the snakelike swimming movements of most sharks. It is one of the few "warm-blooded" sharks. Its elevated body temperature improves muscle efficiency and adds to its swimming power. Florida fishermen have learned that large White Sharks are strong enough to part a cable or chain that has a 3,800-pound breaking strength.

Rows of serrated, razor-sharp teeth of a Great White.

The large pectoral fins are used for banking on turns and for ascent or descent, as well as to provide constant lift for straightaway swimming. The lateral keels ahead of the tail lend balance. When a White Shark swims at the surface, two-thirds of the bladelike dorsal fin protrudes from the water, giving warning of its presence. But the upper tip of the tail remains barely submerged, usually breaking surface only when the shark dives.

A White Shark as large as 20 feet is a rarity, 15-footers are somewhat more common, and 8- to 12-footers are captured or seen frequently. The largest White Shark on record is a giant of 36½ feet in length whose weight is unknown but was probably 12 tons or more. The largest actually weighed, a 21-foot Au-stralian specimen, was over 3½ tons.

White Sharks are mature sexually and able to reproduce at 14 feet. Internal fertilization is accomplished with claspers, the male erectile sex organs. Little is known about the reproductive cycle after fertilization, except that the young are born live and litters are rather small. For example, one 14-foot female was reported as producing a litter of nine pups. At birth, each pup is about 2 feet long. Where and how the offspring live after birth is a mystery, for no White Sharks are seen until they reach a length of 5 or 6 feet.

Adult White Sharks are lone hunters; only the smallest ones regularly feed in groups. They appear to migrate with the season, traveling away from the tropics in summer and returning to them in winter, usually following a prescribed route that brings them to the same place at the same time each year. In Africa and Australia, White Sharks are found in the subtropics or tropics in the winter and in temperate seas in summer, often following mass migrations of prey or the

The twelve-foot bulk of a Great White caught off the shores of Australia.

flow of warm currents to their destinations. The same pattern holds true for both U.S. coasts: White Sharks are reported from New England to Florida and around to Texas on the Atlantic side, and from southern California to Washington on the Pacific side.

In none of their haunts are these solitary sharks abundant; each one seems to require a lot of ocean for itself. In the Florida shark fishery, fewer than 3 out of every 10,000 caught are Great Whites. Peter Gimbel of New York, a shark-hunting Ahab, spent five months searching the world for just one White Shark large enough to star in his movie *Blue Water—White Death*. He finally located his quarry off the south coast of Australia.

The natural food of White Sharks is nearly every type of fish in the sea, plus a variety of mammals and invertebrates. Fish prey include surface swimmers like mackerel and tuna, and bottom species like rockfish and cabezon. Among the invertebrate prey are turtles, squid, and octopus, and among the mammals, sea

lions, seals, dolphins, and sea otters. A large White Shark can swallow an entire animal as large as a sea lion. Many terrestrial animals—goats, horses, cattle, pigs, dogs—that stray or are dumped into the water fall victim to the White Shark. A White Shark has been known to swallow a whole Newfoundland with collar.

Other sharks are also among the favorite foods of the White Shark. A 15½-foot White caught in Florida had two Brown Sharks in its stomach, each one 6 to 7 feet long. Occasionally a shark fisherman has the macabre experience of finding a human hand, leg, rib, or other body part among the assorted contents of a White Shark stomach.

No other shark has a record of so many verified attacks on human beings. The most villainous shark to date, the New Jersey Rogue shark, an 8½-foot White that in July 1916 killed four people along the New Jersey shore in rapid succession and gravely injured a fifth. Too small to swallow a man whole, the shark had bitten off or severely lacerated the legs and feet of each of its victims. The remains of the four victims were snatched from its jaws by various rescuers, as was the fifth victim, a boy who survived. Finally, a fisherman caught and killed a White Shark four miles from Matawan Creek, New Jersey, that was recognized as the attacker by the contents of its stomach—15 pounds of human flesh and bones.

From time to time the Great White Shark has attacked boats without provocation. In July 1953, a shark followed a 12-foot dory fishing out of the port of Forchu, Nova Scotia, for several days, finally the shark attacked the dory, ripped an 8-inch hole in its side, and

Close-up portrait of the most feared shark in the world, taken through the bars of a shark cage.

Off Dangerous Reef, Benchley's cameraman films a Great White.
The steel cage has facilitated the photographing and study of these highly unpredictable maneaters.

sank it. The attacker was identified as a White Shark from a piece of tooth left in the planking.

All the horror stories notwithstanding, the White Shark rarely threatens men. Normally it goes about its affairs ignoring human society completely.

It is difficult to imagine what natural enemies the White Shark might have. Perhaps a large Tiger Shark or a Killer Whale would have the nerve to attack a small White. In fact, the scars of such battles have been found in the flesh of many sharks. Thirteen-year-old Raymond Short of Sydney, Australia, was attacked by

the apparent survivor of just such a contest. Short was swimming 30 yards from Colesdale Beach when he was attacked by an 8-foot-3-inch White Shark. The boy tried to fend off the shark but the fish's grip, first on his thigh and then on his lower right leg, could not be broken. His screams alerted Raymond Joyce, a member of the Colesdale Surf Club, and five other men who attempted unsuccessfully to club the shark. In desperation, the men partially carried and dragged the stricken boy onto the beach, and with him the shark who remained firmly clamped to the boy's leg during the entire rescue. Onshore, the shark's jaws were pried apart, and despite profuse bleeding, lacerations, and tooth marks along the entire length of his shinbone, the boy survived and his leg was saved. (C #1406)

Upon examination, the shark was discovered to have been severely wounded in an attack by another shark of large size. A massive unhealed abdominal wound had the unmistakable imprint of the jaws of a large shark. One wonders if the partial disablement of the shark caused it to attack Short.

There is no commercial fishery for the White Shark because there are too few in any one locale to make a fishery profitable. However, there are concerted White Shark rod-and-reel sport fisheries by fast boat and heavy-duty tackle, both in Australia and along the northeastern coast of the United States. Fighting a White Shark is rugged sport. As one fisherman put it, "It's like being tied into a torpedo in full flight." The largest White taken by rod and reel weighed 2,664 pounds and measured nearly 17 feet in length.

Great White, after striking lure in foreground, remains on the surface and leers at his would-be captors (top left).

Alfred Dean with his record catch of a Great White. Caught off Ceduna, Australia, the shark weighed 2,664 pounds (left)

Some secular and biblical scholars have assigned Jonah to the stomach of a White Shark rather than a whale. The famous animal taxonomist Linnaeus commented on the possibility in the *Septema Naturae* of 1758: "It is likely that the prophet Jonah remained in the belly of this animal [the White Shark] for a space of three days, as Hercules of old did for three nights." I leave the matter to the reader for judgment.

Tiger Shark (galeocerdo cuvieri)

No creature living in the waters of the Caribbean Sea, the Indian Ocean, and around the Australian continent is feared more than the Tiger Shark. It is a notorious man-killer, second only to the White Shark in its yearly toll of victims. The Tiger is a large and powerful creature, armed with the sharpest of teeth and given to haunting shallow beachfronts. It belongs to the Carcharhinid family, which also includes the Great Blue Shark and other typical and often dangerous species. Its Latin name, *Galeocerdo cuvieri,* derives from a Greek word for shark and the name of the French naturalist Cuvier.

The species is named Tiger Shark for the pronounced vertical brown stripes that mark its back and sides rather than for its resemblance in ferocity and carnivorous habits to the jungle tiger. As these sharks age, their stripes become lighter, gradually fading into the grayish-brown color of the hide. In the oldest ones, they show very faintly, making identification difficult from any distance. The underside is a pale grayish white.

About 2 feet long at birth, the Tiger Shark grows to 10 to 15 feet by middle age. Giants of the species probably reach 20 feet or longer, but so far the largest actually recorded is 18 feet. The largest Tiger taken on rod and reel was 13 feet 10½ inches long and weighed 1,780 pounds (caught at Cherry Grove, South Carolina, in June 1964). Slender when young, Tigers become heavy in the midsection with advancing age. The fins are large and stout. The tail is sickle-shaped and the upper lobe is exceptionally long, almost half the length of the body. A lateral keel projects from each side of the body near the tail. The head and the eyes are large. The snout is blunt and squarish. The

A twelve-hundred-pound Tiger shark.

mouth is underslung in typical shark fashion.

The teeth of the Tiger Shark are unique in form. They are sharp, thin, and serrated; broad at the base with convex edges narrowing to a low, swept back tip. The rearward edge curves downward to form a notch halfway from tip to base. The front row of teeth is backed by several rows of replacement teeth. Ichthyologists familiar with this uniquely formed tooth can identify the Tiger Shark as the attacker from the appearance of the wounds in a victim.

Because of the swept-back tips of the teeth, the jaws of the Tiger Shark are well equipped for seizing and holding prey. The sharpness of the teeth enables the shark to chop pieces from very large victims. The jaws are suspended by elastic supports so that they protrude and open widely, which permits the shark to swallow very large prey whole.

All its armament notwithstanding, the species is a super scavenger, totally lacking in dietary discrimination. Furthermore, it is a sluggish creature that avoids light and prowls at night. It feeds on any edible creature and also ingests a wide assortment of flotsam and jetsam. Animals that have been found in Tiger Shark stomachs include hundreds of species of fish, dozens of other types of sharks, crabs, sea lions, turtles, dolphins, conchs, squids, sea birds, a whole spaniel dog, and parts of horses, cows, sheep, and human beings. Among the normally inedible objects found in this shark's innards are canned goods, items of clothing, a leather wallet, a coil of copper wire, a driver's license, a sack of coal, and an 18-pound tom-tom.

One summer night on a research mission to the Hudson Canyon off the entrance to New York Harbor, we caught a 12-foot Tiger Shark that weighed half a ton and had a stomachful of New York City garbage. City wastes dumped into the water had attracted this monster to feed in the canyon located between Coney Island, New York, and Sandy Hook, New Jersey. During the remainder of the summer we caught from our research vessel, the *Dolphin,* 28 more Tiger Sharks in the general vicinity, along with 239 other sharks of such dangerous species as the Hammerhead, Great White, and Mako.

The sensory mechanisms of the Tiger Shark are typical of those of the whole shark tribe. They have a sharp sense of smell and good sound perception. Their vision is only passable, however, and they probably have no color perception. However, in dim light they undoubtedly see as well as any fish. Consequently, they spend their days in deeper water and come to the surface to feed at night.

From research, we know that the Tiger, like many species of the shark tribe, is especially alert to any signal of a prey in a weakened state. Behavioral scientist T. W. Brown was able to attract a Tiger in the wild by playing back recorded sounds of wounded, thrashing reef fishes. It took the Tiger only twelve minutes to hear and recognize the sounds and to arrive at the underwater speaker from an unknown distance away.

It may be that the Tiger is not as cannibalistic as the other species of large sharks. If it were, one would expect to find a social order to limit cannibalism, but the small mingle with the large and the females with the males. Nor do there appear to be any special coastal sanctuaries, or nurseries, for the newly-born young, as is typical of so many shark species. Perhaps it is because of the extra hazards and high mortality during babyhood in the open sea that litters are so numerous—large females bear as many as eighty live young, each about 2½ feet long. Copulation is accomplished by the intrusion of the paired claspers of the male into the paired female organ.

Tiger Sharks are found throughout the warmer waters of the world ocean, wherever the temperature is 70° F. or higher. But nowhere do they occur in great abundance. Their range includes Australia, Africa, Hawaii, southern California, and the Atlantic coast of the Americas from southern New England to Brazil (including the West Indies). Tiger Sharks inhabit coastal waters from the littoral shallows to the offshore deeps and reefs. They appear to be attracted to populated shores, perhaps to scavenge city wastes thrown into the water.

Tiger Sharks are nowhere abundant enough to make for a profitable fishery, but they are a real prize when taken by fishermen who are out for other sharks. Tiger skin finds a ready market because it is durable and tough, having six to ten times the tensile strength of ox hide. The liver was valuable for vitamins and

*The opened jaws of a huge Tiger
— always an awesome sight.*

medicinals in the days before they were so cheaply synthesized. The flesh is used rarely for human consumption.

The Tiger revenges itself by attacking boats and swimmers. It is one of the few shark species known to attack boats, but usually does so only when provoked by a fisherman. The most violent of such attacks occurred in Florida waters, half a mile off Palm Beach, in February 1948, when a Tiger Shark estimated to be 15 to 18 feet long struck a 28-foot motor craft with enough force to sink it on the spot. Fortunately the occupants were rescued by another boat before their craft went under.

The Tiger Shark ranks second only to the Great White in the frequency with which it attacks man, and it is the leading menace in the coastal waters of Australia, India, and the state of Florida. Although the records show only twenty-seven verified attacks, the Tiger is the probable villain in several hundred more. In many cases where the Tiger Shark has been positively identified as the attacker, human remains were found in the stomachs of captured specimens. For example, an 11½-foot Tiger Shark was positively identified as the attacker of two young men, Jack Brinkley and Norman Girvan, because the day after the attack a specimen was caught that had pieces of arms and legs in it, among which was Girvan's right hand, recognizable by a distinctive scar. The two had been surfing at Coolangatta, New South Wales, Australia, on October 23, 1937, when the shark struck. (C #37)

The squared snout is an unmistakable trait of the Tiger shark.

One of the most vicious attacks by a Tiger Shark was recorded in the Pamperin case. A routine day of abalone fishing off La Jolla Cove, California, became the last for skin diver Robert Pamperin. On June 14, 1959, he and a buddy were searching for abalone on the seabed some 150 feet from the shore when suddenly Pamperin shot from the water, screaming for help, and then just as suddenly disappeared from sight. His buddy, 60 feet away on the surface, raced to the spot where Pamperin had just vanished and through his faceplate saw the terrifying spectacle of a fellow diver half protruding from the mouth of a 20-foot Tiger Shark in a cloud of blood. Failing to frighten the shark from finishing its deadly task, he fled to shore to warn other swimmers out of the water. Despite extensive searches by scuba divers and helicopters, no trace of Pamperin was ever found. The Tiger Shark had been thorough. (C #376)

Of the numerous stories about the stomach contents of Tiger Sharks, the most incredible is from the Coogee Aquarium in Australia. On April 18, 1935, the aquarium crew brought in and revived a 14-foot Tiger Shark that had become tangled in their set lines after swallowing a smaller shark caught fair on a hook.

After six days in the aquarium tank, the Tiger vomited up a tattooed human arm with a rope tied by a seaman's knot around the wrist. Curiously, the arm appeared to be fresh and little digested after what must have been at least a week in the shark's stomach.

At first the arm was believed to have come from a suicide. However, an unusual tattoo of two boxers and a routine fingerprint check identified the arm as that of a local gangster, James Smith, who had disappeared under mysterious circumstances and who, it appeared, was murdered, dismembered, and thrown into the sea. The arm had been so cleanly cut at the shoulder that the shark could not have bitten it off.

The arm was carefully preserved, according to the Sydney *Morning Herald,* and presented to the coroner, who proclaimed he would "not assume that

Though closely related to the Lemon shark, the Bull shark has a broader, more rounded head and is more sluggish in its movements.

the man is dead until other parts of his body have been found." But in spite of an intensive search, the rest of the body was not found.

Police investigation led to a Patrick Brady, who had rented a cottage with the murdered man in early April and was the last person seen in his company. Brady was arrested for murder on May 17.

Three days later, a material witness with an unexplained 32-caliber bullet wound in his head led police on a four-hour chase around Sydney harbor before being captured. Babbling incoherently, "Jimmy Smith is dead, I'm nearly dead, and there is only one other left," the wounded man, wealthy Reginald William Holmes, a Sydney boat builder and friend of Mrs. Smith, was taken to a hospital. All he would admit was that he had lent Smith money for business purposes. Released on June 12, he lived only until evening. A suspect was arrested and then discharged, after a hearing, as not guilty.

After much more evidence had been heard in the case of Patrick Brady, an order was issued to restrain the coroner from continuing his inquiry. Based on a statute of 1276, the court ruled that "a single limb could not be considered a corpus delicti" and that "no inquest could be held without a corpus delicti." By September, Brady had been cleared of all charges in the murder of Smith and the case was dismissed.

But the Tiger Shark, which itself lived only two days after disgorging the arm, had not revealed the whole story. Numerous rumors related the case to insurance money withheld, drug trafficking among the eminent, gangsters, yachts, and an official hush-up of the facts to protect those involved. Whatever the real motive, the case of the Shark Arm Murders remains unsolved.

Bull Shark (carcharhinus)

The Bull Shark group is unique in that it embraces species that inhabit both fresh and salt water. Bull Sharks are found along tropical and subtropical coasts of much of the world ocean—Africa, the Indian Ocean, Australia, the East Indies, and the western Atlantic from southeastern United States to Brazil.

Prominent members of the group are the Lake Nicaragua Shark, the Zambezi Shark (South Africa), and the Bull or Cub Shark (U.S. Atlantic).

Bull Sharks are distinguished by their wide head and blunt, rounded snout. The body is heavy and its form compact, featuring a prominent first dorsal fin that is triangular in shape. The eye is small and piglike and the skin is light to dark gray above and white below, with no conspicuous fin markings. The species reaches a length of 10 feet and a weight of over 400 pounds, but a Bull Shark of only 6 or 7 feet can easily dismember and kill an adult person.

The upper teeth of the Bull Shark are coarsely serrated and broadly triangular. The lower teeth are serrated and triangular, but more slender than the teeth of the upper jaw.

Dr. David Davies, an expert on Zambezi Sharks (as Bulls are called in South Africa), considers them to be "rather slow-swimming sharks which frequent shallow inshore areas, estuaries, or rivers." But still he terms them an "extremely aggressive species which is capable of moving fast and making fearful attacks on large fish, including other sharks of similar size."

The Zambezi Shark invades the Natal coast of South Africa in the late spring each year (November–December) to commence an annual campaign of violence that lasts until summer's end (April). The typical pattern is a sudden attack on a wader in waist-deep water—exemplified by the fate of Barbara Strauss on December 29, 1963. Strauss, a medical student, was bathing waist-deep in the 73.4°F. surf of the Natal north coast at 2:00 P.M. Along with two others, she saw the 6-foot Zambezi Shark charging toward her. It scraped the others in passing and struck hard, dragging the screaming Strauss underwater. It attacked twice again before the victim could be rescued and carried to the beach. The right hand had been severed at the wrist, the right foot chopped off above the ankle, and an extensive hunk taken from the right buttock. Emergency measures at the scene and the rapid arrival of her father, a physician, saved her life.

Because they haunt the shallow estuarine shores and rivers of highly populated areas around the world, Bull Sharks doubtless encounter and kill more people than any other species of shark, although positive identifications are rare. The apparent toll has gone as high as thirty-five attacks per year around the mouth of one river, the Devi in India. The notorious "Ganges Shark" is of the Bull Shark group.

A typical invasion from the sea was reported by three canoeists on the Limpopo River who encountered Bull Sharks 120 miles upriver from the Mozambique coast. Sharks up to 8 feet in length repeatedly charged the canoes, bumping them with their snouts. Jopie Overes' canoe was ripped open but he was able to safely land the sinking craft on shore.

Bull Sharks also live in inland lakes such as Lake Nicaragua and Lake Maracaibo (Venezuela), where they are greatly feared because of their propensity to attack in very shallow water. Bull Sharks are also found in Lake Okeechobee in interior Florida, where they swim in from their normal haunts in the sea, but no attack has been reported there. Their very presence in such isolated freshwater bodies is a curious paradox so far unresolved by ichthyologists.

Bulls are the commonest of all sharks off the west coast of Florida, and, according to my colleague Eugenie Clark, are there in abundance year-round. Thus, the same species of shark that in South Africa is a notorious attacker has also claimed victims in the waters of Florida. My opinion, confirmed by knowledgeable Floridians, is that many of these 27 attacks were by Bull Sharks, though positive identification is lacking.

The Bull Shark is notorious for violent shallow-water attacks in the Caribbean too, as shown in the case of A. J. Eggink, which was reported by my colleague John E. Randall. On March 30, 1952, Eggink rushed to the rescue of a child menaced by a shark in the shallow waters of a Curacao bathing beach. The rescuer had waded into a depth of 4 to 5 feet when the shark struck once, removing a large chunk from his buttock. By now, other rescuers arrived, and while they dragged Eggink to safety, the huge 9-foot shark trailed its victim through the blood-stained waters right to the beach. The shark was captured by hand and dragged out on the sand. The victim survived—but spent six months in the hospital.

Whaler Shark (carcharhinus)

Whaler Sharks are the number-one scourge of Australian waters. The U.S. Navy Official Shark File credits the Whaler Shark with twenty verified attacks, in which the Bronze Whaler was the certain culprit in eight and the Black Whaler in one. A high proportion of the eleven nonattributed attacks were probably by the Black Whaler, since despite the statistics, it has the reputation in Australia as a far more notorious man-killer than the Bronze.

The Whaler Shark is part of a large family of sharks, the Requiem Sharks or *Carcharhinidae*, that includes the Bull, Tiger, Lemon, and Blue. The two species of particular interest are the Bronze Whaler and Black Whaler, both of whom are abundant off the Australian east coast.

The Black Whaler grows to about 12 feet in length and 1,000 pounds in weight, and the Bronze grows to 10 feet and about 700 pounds. Both have a light belly and a dark back, but the Black Whaler is a dark gray above, while the Bronze is a bright coppery bronze.

Whaler Sharks are trim and streamlined in shape, with an exceptionally high upper tail lobe. The teeth of the two species are similar, being saw-edged, very sharp, and in the form of triangles with flared bases.

Whalers were given their name by Australian whalemen of the last century, whose company they often kept during expeditions from New South Wales, but not in a spirit of camaraderie. The sharks attacked and ate parts of the carcasses of whales being towed to the factories ashore, thus robbing the whalemen of much of their profit.

Whaler Sharks have more serious crimes on their record, as illustrated by the attack on young Geoffrey Corner south of Adelaide, Australia, on December 9, 1962. Taking part in a spearfishing contest, Corner had surfaced close to the orange float that held his catch. He was just heading down again when a Bronze Whaler struck. As the shark sank its teeth into his right leg, Corner lashed out with a spear, but only succeeded in impaling his other leg. A surfer 10 yards away came rapidly to his aid, beat the shark off with a paddle, draped Corner over the surfboard, and pulled the spear out of his leg. He quickly stabbed the shark and towed the victim to shallow water. But in spite of his rescuer's prompt and courageous action, Corner was too badly injured to survive. (C #1122)

The very next month a Whaler attacked a young Sydney actress, Marcia Hathaway, in the knee-deep water of Sugarloaf Bay. She was gathering oysters with her fiancé when he heard her scream. "I turned around to see her being dragged into deeper water. I raced to her, caught her arms, and began a tug-of-war with the shark holding her." Astride the fish, he punched and kicked and finally succeeded in driving it off with help from a second man. Loading her into a boat, they "tried to put a tourniquet on her leg, but it was too badly torn to be able to do anything, with deep wounds running its entire length." An ambulance was waiting when the trio reached the boatshed, but it burned out its clutch before it reached the highway. The actress died before a second ambulance got her to the hospital.

Sand Tiger Shark (odontaspis)

The group of Sand Tigers includes similar sharks found in different parts of the world and is not to be confused with the Tiger Shark. All are of the genus *Odontaspis,* and whether it has two, four, or more species is still being debated by taxonomists. It is agreed that the Ragged Tooth Shark of Africa and the Sand Tiger Shark of the American east coast are the same species, *taurus.* The Grey Nurse Shark of Australia may be a different species, and has been given the Latin name *arenarius.* Various members of the group also live in the East Indies area and in the Atlantic off Brazil. Wherever they occur, Sand Tigers are a potential threat to swimmers.

The Sand Tiger has the sharp pointed teeth typical of some of the most ferocious species. It has the jaws, eyes, and body shape of the man-killers, and since it is the most "sharklike" of sharks, it arouses primal fears. Aquarium directors, impressed with its look of menace and its adaptability to tank life, have made the Sand Tiger the most popular of all exhibit sharks.

Sand Tigers have flat heads, toothy underslung mouths, and broad powerful tails. They have the spots of the leopard rather than the stripes of their namesake. They are slender creatures which at maximum length of 11 feet weigh but 700 pounds, or about half the weight of a Tiger Shark of equal length. The usual size is about 6½ feet and 225 pounds.

The teeth of the Sand Tiger Shark are long, sharp, nonserrated, and stacked row behind row in both upper and lower jaws like bayonets at the ready. These teeth are designed for seizing prey that is to be swallowed whole and not for cutting or tearing. Equipped in this fashion, Sand Tigers are deadly efficient predators that successfully raid schools of the fastest species of coastal fishes such as the bluefish (called Shad in South Africa, tailor in Australia).

The appetite of this shark is nearly insatiable. Sand Tigers seem to be seeking food continuously, stalking their prey day and night. Almost all shallow-water species—butterfish, flounders, menhaden, bonito, lobster, crabs—are victims of this aggressive

(Above) Ragged Tooth shark biting prey.

Sand Tigers

predator. While they are usually free-lance feeders, Sand Tigers occasionally hunt cooperatively in large packs. Ichthyologist R. J. Coles reported at the proceedings of the Biological Society of Washington, "On one occasion I saw a school of a hundred or more surround a school of bluefish and force them into a solid mass in shallow water, and then at the same instant the entire school of sharks dashed in on the bluefish."

Sand Tigers are best adapted for feeding in shallow waters of less than 30 feet where small schooling coastal fishes abound. Their body shape, fins, and tail are designed for the combination of maneuverability and sudden bursts of speed needed for optimum performance in this shore zone. In contrast to most sharks, Sand Tigers can achieve buoyancy by ingesting air into their stomachs, thus avoiding the need to expend energy merely to stay afloat.

The young are born live, one or two at a time, after a gestation period of up to twenty-two months. They are predators before they are born—the most developed young in the uterus prey actively on the thousands of yet undeveloped pea-sized eggs. Born at a length of 36 inches (larger than young White Sharks), they are well prepared for survival from the moment of birth.

It is curious that the Sand Tiger has never been known to make an unprovoked attack on man in U.S. waters, whereas it is considered to be a really serious menace in South Africa, 19 verified attacks, and Australia, 11 verified attacks. Most of the shallow-water shark attacks in South Africa are attributed to Ragged Tooth Sharks, the African variety of this species. According to the late ichthyologist, J. L. B. Smith, "If an unwary bather approaches within reach there is a savage rush, and usually another fatality. Even if the victim escapes, the terrible teeth cause fearful lacerations." Yet I have been unable to find any official records detailing a specific attack by a Ragged Tooth Shark.

There is little commercial value to this shark, although the skin is used to a limited extent in the manufacture of leather and occasionally the flesh is eaten. However, each of the dozens of specimens delivered alive for exhibit in commercial aquariums is worth many hundreds of dollars.

Commercial fishermen loathe the Sand Tiger Shark's frequent habit of attacking nets full of fish. Such attacks lead to shredded gear, lost catches, and trips to port for new nets. According to shark angling experts Frank Mundus and William Wisner, if you can catch them, Sand Tigers "provide lively action on light shark-fishing tackle." While they are voracious feeders, they have an unsharklike reluctance to take the baited hook of the angler.

The Mako (isurus oxyrinchus) and Porbeagle (lamna nasus)

The Mako and Porbeagle are closely related in appearance and have similar life styles. They are both near relatives of the White Shark, and the three together make up the family of mackerel sharks, *Lamnidae*. The Mako is a warm-water species and a favorite of deep-sea sport fishermen. The Porbeagle (also called the Mackerel Shark) is a cold-water species and the object of a prosperous commercial fishery.

Both species share with the White Shark the ability to elevate body temperatures to improve muscle efficiency; they are in this way "warm-blooded." The Mako is notorious for attacking humans and their boats. While considered potentially dangerous, the Porbeagle thus far has proved relatively peaceful.

The scientific name of the Mako translates as "symmetrical-tail" (*isurus*) "sharp-snout" (*oxyrinchus*) shark. The Porbeagle is named after a horrible maneating animal (*Lamna*) that Greek parents invented to intimidate naughty children (*nasus* means nose).

Both species are blue-gray on the upper body, though the Mako tends more toward a bright blue. On both the color changes abruptly to white halfway down the flanks.

These sharks are aggressive open-ocean predators and their bodies are styled for high speed. A Mako can run down and kill a swordfish, a swift ocean species capable of speeds up to 60 miles per hour. Like their White Shark cousin, these two species are torpedo-shaped and finely tapered fore and aft. They both have dorsal and pectoral fins that are stout and broad, with symmetrical tunalike tails of large size and great

strength. The Mako is slimmer than the Porbeagle when young, but soon catches up in heftiness. At 10 feet long, the Mako may weigh 900 pounds, outweighing the Porbeagle by several hundred pounds.

The mouth of each species is set well back under the sharply pointed snout in both species. The strong jaws are protrusible, enabling these sharks to open their mouths to a jaw angle of about 90 degrees where the teeth can function most efficiently. Several rows of teeth are in use simultaneously.

Both species have teeth designed to seize and hold prey, not to dismember it. The Mako's teeth are long, sharp, fanglike, and curved strongly backwards. The Porbeagle's are similar, but are tricuspid, each tooth having a smaller secondary point growing up on each side of the main shaft. This difference in tooth structure makes it easy to tell the Mako from the Porbeagle.

Unlike the White Shark's teeth, the edges of the teeth of Mako and Porbeagle Sharks are smooth, not sharp or saw-edged. These teeth were once highly prized for earrings by the Maoris of New Zealand, who caught the Mako by putting a noose around its tail.

Their dentition suits these two species admirably for hunting small prey, but not as well for feeding on large prey they can't swallow whole. However, there is on record a Mako of 720 pounds that swallowed a whole swordfish weighing 110 pounds (after biting off its tail). Then, too, packs of Makos have been seen to attack a large swordfish and bite out individual pieces of flesh. In *The Old Man and the Sea,* Ernest Hemingway wrote: "This was a fish built to feed on all the fishes in the sea, that were so fast and strong and well armed that they had no other enemy. . . . When the old man saw him coming he knew that this was a shark that had no fear at all and would do exactly what he wished. . . ."

Normally the Mako feeds on squid and small schooling fishes like mackerel, menhaden, and herring, as well as dogfish sharks and other bottom fishes.

Gaffed by fishermen,
an angry Mako shark
displays its daggerlike teeth.

The Porbeagle is not such a ferocious feeder, but like the Mako, it will prey on schooling surface fishes. Porbeagles specialize in going deep in the sea to feed on squid and to hunt for bottom fishes like flounder, haddock, or cod.

The Mako ranges widely in the Atlantic, from the North Sea to the Mediterranean and South Africa, and from southern New England to Brazil. In the Pacific, the Mako is found in the Indo-Pacific region and around New Zealand and Australia.

(Marineland of Florida)

The Porbeagle usually inhabits waters colder than 65°F. In the Atlantic, it ranges from Norway to North Africa and from Newfoundland to New Jersey. In the Pacific, it ranges from southern Alaska to northern California, from Kamchatka to Japan, and around New Zealand to Japan and Australia.

In each species, the young are born live and are about 2 feet long at birth. Porbeagles bear litters of one to four pups; Makos from two to five (occasionally up to ten). Internal fertilization is accomplished by the erectile claspers of the male.

Porbeagles do not inhabit shallow waters and therefore seldom threaten swimmers or divers. I know of two attacks by the species, one of which was fatal: Maurizio Sarra, a twenty-eight-year-old Italian diver, lost his life on the west coast of Italy on September 22, 1962, after having been attacked by a shark that ap-

Because of its tail structure and pointed snout, the Mako closely resembles the Great White.

pears to have been a Porbeagle. The attack took place 30 feet underwater. Sarra was harpooning and manipulating a grouper at the time, and blood and mucus were spread all over him.

While the Mako is primarily a deep-water shark, it has been identified as the culprit in certain beach-front attacks on swimmers. The Mako is more notorious, perhaps, for attacking boats and is often listed as savage and dangerous. A pack of Makos is blamed for ramming and sinking a small boat off Bellami Reef, Australia, and for devouring at least one, and possibly three, of the four occupants. Castaways, it would appear, have reason to fear both the Mako and the Porbeagle.

In recent years, Norwegian fishermen have caught up to 9 million pounds of Porbeagle annually, much of it coming from New England and Canadian waters. The gear used is the longline—baited hooks fastened at intervals to a single heavy line dozens of miles long suspended in the water by floats. The object is shark meat, which is frozen and exported, mostly to Italy. A Porbeagle steak resembles swordfish closely in taste and texture. The species is also taken on rod and reel. The angling record (1965) is held by a fisherman in Long Island, New York: a Porbeagle 7 feet 9½ inches in length and weighing 400 pounds.

Mako meat is also very tasty, but the shark's distribution and habits preclude it as a target for commercial fisheries. Nevertheless, it is much sought after by deep-sea anglers because of its speed, gameness, and antics. The record size for a rod-and-reel catch is a 12-foot Mako weighing 1,000 pounds that was caught at Mayor Island, New Zealand, in 1943.
Zane Grey, another Mako fan, called the species ''a premier sporting fish, as game as beautiful, as ferocious as enduring.''

Hammerhead Shark (sphyrnidae)

The Hammerhead group is distinguished from all other sharks by the strange ''hammer'' shape of its head. Taxonomically, the group is divided into nine species of the genus *Sphyrnidae* (meaning ''hammer''). Three large species occur worldwide in warm and temperate waters—the Bronze Hammerhead, the Common Hammerhead, and the Great Hammerhead.

Although in all other respects a typical-looking shark, each Hammerhead is fitted out with a curious flat, wing-shaped appendage on the end of the snout,

*The odd-looking Hammerheads, which steer by their long noses
and have magnificent stereoscopic vision, are among the best predators.*

Hammerhead shark breaking the surface.

in front of the mouth. The eyes and nostrils are placed far apart at the outer ends of this hammer, giving the shark an advantage in visual and perhaps olfactory perception. The hammer also probably serves as a planing device which gives Hammerheads a rapid steering response where it is most needed for closing in on prey—right at the mouth. In spite of these possibilities, ichthyologists do not yet agree that one, or any, of these advantages sufficiently justifies this strange adaptation.

Hammerheads normally grow to lengths of 5 to 15 feet, depending upon the species, but there is on record a Great Hammerhead of 18 feet 4 inches. Pectoral and dorsal fins are large and roughly triangular; other fins are modest. The tail is symmetrical and powerful, with a very long upper lobe.

Hammerhead Sharks prefer shallow coastal waters for the most part. They feed heavily on bottom life, eating some shrimps, crabs, and other shellfish, but mostly smaller fishes, squids, and the like. They have a particular liking for sting rays, which they ingest in

quantity, notwithstanding the troublesome tail sting, which would easily damage the eyes of a typical shark. The sting is ineffectual against the Hammerhead, whose eyes are protected from damage because they are far out on the ends of the hammer and away from the mouth. In a large specimen, the distance from eye to eye may be 3 feet. So heavily do Hammerheads prey on sting rays that no less than fifty "stings" were found imbedded in the head and back of a 13½-foot specimen caught off North Carolina.

Hammerheads are warm-water sharks that move north along the American coasts in the summer. In American waters, the Bronze Hammerhead is found south of New Jersey on the Atlantic side, and off southern California on the Pacific side. The Common Hammerhead occurs along the east coast north to southern Nova Scotia and also in southern California. The Great Hammerhead ranges north to North Carolina in the Atlantic but does not inhabit the Pacific side. Hammerheads often occur in great abundance in their favorite feeding spots, migrating there in large loose schools. A school of more than 1,000 Smooth Hammerheads migrating northward were once sighted off Cape Hatteras, North Carolina.

Hammerheads are dangerous sharks, with thirteen verified attacks on their record. In American waters, the greatest threat from Hammerheads appears to be off Florida and southern California. Like many other sharks, Hammerheads often leave the deeper ocean and move up onto the shallow reefs in the evening. My own encounter with a Hammerhead in the Florida Keys, in April 1971, proved the wisdom of the local diver's rule: "Sundown, divers up." I had forgotten all about time until I realized it was becoming dark underwater. Aware of the danger I started back, scanning the depths for sharks. To get to the boat meant swimming along a 20-foot deep channel that rose up from the deeper ocean gulf stream waters—shark territory. Then, right below me, swimming near the bottom of the channel came a Hammerhead shark, about twelve feet in length with three feet of hammer. The shark noticed me and began to reverse course with a quick

roll of the snout, head, and shoulders. Fortunately, I was near enough to my boat to swim to safety before it could manage to reach me.

Gertrude Holaday was not so lucky at West Palm Beach, Florida, on September 21, 1931. Only about 200 feet from shore, Holaday was struck by a shark in full view of bathers and lifeguard. The shark followed the girl in the blood-clouded water as she struggled to reach the lifeguard, who had plunged in to rescue her. At his approach, the shark retreated, but remained for a time in the shallow water. The victim had gouges up to 10 inches long taken out of her right thigh and calf. According to the lifeguard, the shark was an 8-foot Hammerhead. (C #217)

The diver's skill at self-defense is well illustrated by the Hammerhead attack on Kenney Ruszenas on August 22, 1964. The 10- to 12-foot Hammerhead had sighted Ruszenas as he dived into 40 feet of water near Palm Beach, Florida. In a direct run, the shark closed on its prey, at a 45-degree angle, mouth opening wider as it approached. Ruszenas, thrusting his spear gun against the underside of the shark's broad head, lifted and forced the attacker to pass over him. The persistent Hammerhead wheeled and hurled itself at the diver again, this time at chest level. When his spear gun slid off the shark's flat snout, the resourceful diver managed to turn the fish aside using only his hands. The shark then disappeared as suddenly as it had come.

Fishermen are wary about attempting to harpoon a Hammerhead because it will often ram a boat in rage, and a large one has the power to capsize a fisherman's craft. The Common Hammerhead is quite dangerous in this respect.

Hammerheads are sought for their hides, which are thin but tough and make a durable and handsome leather. The flesh is not desirable. Many Hammerheads are caught for sport by surf anglers and boat fishermen each year.

Thresher Shark (olopias vulpinus)

Among the whole tribe of sharks there is one member, the Thresher, whose distinctive feature is its tail rather than its teeth. Attached to the end of this shark is a tail of extraordinary size—a tail whose length equals that of the rest of the body.

The Thresher is of moderate length, robust in build, and streamlined in the manner of the hunting sharks (those that prey on fast-moving bait fishes). The flat, triangular teeth are smaller than those of most sharks. The Thresher does not rip and chew hunks from large prey and therefore it needs teeth only to retain within its mouth the schooling bait fishes upon which it preys. In keeping with its habit of feeding on small prey, its mouth is comparatively small.

In body form, the Thresher resembles the Porbeagle, being torpedo-shaped with a small head and short snout. The pectoral fins are long, broad, and sickle-shaped to provide the means for rapid and accurate maneuvers at close range. The Thresher is a dark grayish brown to black above, shading through grays to whites on the belly side.

Although we have heard of a Thresher Shark 20 feet long, one as long as 14 feet is unusual and most of those caught or sighted are 12 feet or less. Because half its length is tail, a 12-foot Thresher is a lightweight compared to a short-tail shark of the same length. For example, a 12-foot Thresher weighs only 300 to 400 pounds, while a 12-foot Mako weighs 1,000 to 1,200 pounds or more.

The family of Thresher Sharks, *Alopidae*, is a small one. Of the six species proposed by various taxonomists, five are either rare, confined to deep parts of the ocean, or unproved as separate species. The one noteworthy species is *Alopias vulpinus*, which we call simply the Thresher Shark. As often happens with animals, the Thresher has a double Latin name. *Alopias* is from the Greek *alopex*, and *vulpinus* is from the Latin *vulpes*. Both mean fox. Experts cannot agree on whether the reference is to the Thresher's cunning or to its long, and thus foxlike, tail. I favor the "tail theory" because this shark gets along less by its cleverness than by the forceful and energetic use of its sickle-shaped tail.

The tail is used in the hunting of small bait fish that school in surface waters such as herring, pilchards, and mackerel. From eyewitness accounts, the Thresher typically locates prey fish at the surface, then drives them into a compact school by circling around and flailing the surface of the water with rapid, threshing strokes of its tail. Once the bait fish are herded up, the Thresher closes in for the kill, striking accurately at the crowded and panicked mass, stunning several of the bait fishes, and finally releasing the rest of the school. It devours the injured and dazed specimens as the rest flee to safety.

But sometimes the Thresher takes on a single prey, as described by W. E. Allen in Frank Mundus and Bill Wisner's *Sport Fishing for Sharks*:

> I noticed a small fish . . . frantically swimming . . . a moment later the pursuer, a six-foot Thresher Shark, passed partly ahead of the victim . . . when it turned quickly and gave the coach-whip lash with the tail which I had seen before. . . . It then became evident that the victim was seriously injured. . . . I was much impressed with the accuracy shown in its strokes at a single flying target.

Some experts are not so impressed. In his book, *The Life of Sharks*, my colleague Paul Budker states cynically that

> If it were deprived of its cumbersome appendage, the Thresher would hardly die of starvation. There seems to be no doubt that it could do just as well as related species without somersaults and other antics and without behaving like a sheep dog

Yet the Thresher's chief distinctions are its flamboyant tail and dazzling feeding tactics.

Knowledge about the reproduction of Threshers is very sparse. Females reach maturity at a length of about 14 feet. Thereafter, they produce litters of two to four pups each. The male is equipped with twin copulatory organs, the claspers, by which sperm are deposited within the female. The fertilized eggs hatch in the oviducts and the young live and grow in the uterus of the mother. Delivery occurs after a gestation period of several months. At birth the young are 4 to 5 feet in length and probably quite capable of caring for themselves, although one comes across an occasional old report suggesting that the mothers remain close to their young and protect them for some time after they are born.

This species lives in both the Pacific and Atlantic oceans and in the northern and southern hemispheres. It is found in temperate and subtropical waters, wherever and whenever there is an ample supply of schooling bait fishes. But nowhere does the Thresher occur in abundance. It is a highly specialized shark, and prospers only by taking advantage of special circumstances that are in its favor. It appears to migrate great distances, to temperate waters in summer and back to subtropical waters in winter.

Australian underwater photographer Ben Cropp riding a thirty-five-foot Whale shark.

In the Atlantic, Thresher Sharks are reported from Europe to Africa, and in the Americas from Canada to Florida, and Brazil to Argentina. In the Pacific, they occur from northern Washington to southern California, and from Panama to Chile. They do not appear in truly tropical waters. While Threshers are commonly reported from Australia and occur in the Indian Ocean, they do not seem to frequent the Asian side of the Pacific.

Although there appears to be no commercial market for its meat, sport fishermen who have tried Thresher Shark claim it is good eating.

Thresher Sharks do not attack man—for that matter anything larger than a mackerel—because of their small mouth, small teeth, and general behavior.

Whale Shark
(rhincodon typus)
and Basking Shark
(cetorhinus maximus)

These two sharks exemplify a curious contradiction of nature: that the largest species are frequently the least ferocious. The Basking Shark and the Whale Shark are grazers rather than predators. They grow to massive size by consuming huge quantities of the abundant, drifting planktonic life of the sea. A docile manner is compatible with their peaceable mode of life.

The Whale Shark is the world's largest fish, reaching a length of 50 feet or more. A specimen of 35 feet weighs 10 tons and one of 50 feet weighs upwards of 25 tons.

The Basking Shark is the world's second largest fish, reaching a length of 40 feet or more. The recorded weight of a typical 30-foot specimen is 13,000 pounds divided as follows (not including 1,000 pounds of food in its stomach):

Head	2,000 pounds
Liver	2,000 pounds
Fins	2,000 pounds
Tail	1,000 pounds
Skin	2,000 pounds
Flesh	3,000 pounds
Organs	1,000 pounds

The Whale Shark is aptly named, not only because of its massive size but also because its body shape is more whalelike than sharklike. It has a large head and thick shoulders that taper sharply to a broad tail. Its color ranges from dark gray to reddish and greenish brown overlaid with light spots on the head and back and vertical stripes on the sides. The species is unique among sharks in having a series of pronounced ridges that start behind the head and run the length of the back.

The Basking Shark, which has a smaller head and thicker midsection, is more typically sharklike in appearance. It is dark on the back and paler on the belly. This otherwise plain shark is distinguished by exceptionally long gill slits necessitated by the great volumes of water it must strain in feeding.

It has been calculated that a 23-foot Basking Shark strains 40,000 gallons of seawater through its mouth in five minutes while cruising at a speed of 2 knots. The planktonic creatures that make up the diet of Whale and Basking sharks are removed from the water by a grating of gill rakers. These structures extend across the throat to serve as an efficient sieve to hold the food as the water passes through the mouth and out the gills. Before hibernating at the ocean bottom to save energy during the winter scarcity of food, Basking Sharks often shed their gill rakers.

Although most other sharks are so heavy they must swim constantly to avoid sinking, Basking and Whale sharks are buoyant enough to spend considerable time resting, or basking, at the surface. This buoyancy is provided by their enormous oily livers.

Whale and Basking sharks rarely compete with each other for food or space because they inhabit different latitudes. The Whale Shark frequents warmer tropical waters, while the Basking Shark is seen in colder temperate and subarctic waters. Each species is found on both the Atlantic and Pacific coasts of the United States. Both appear to migrate north and south with the seasons.

Fishermen from Norway, Japan, Great Britain, and other countries have harpooned Whale and Basking sharks for their liver oil and meat. The liver of a large Basking Shark yields up to 600 gallons of oil. Presently such fisheries are not commercially important because of low market demand and the depletion of shark populations from overfishing.

Neither species deliberately attacks man, although both are potential hazards to marine traffic when resting at the surface because of their bulk and sluggishness. Basking Sharks appear more agile than Whale Sharks, which have been the victim of many recorded collisions. The hazard is illustrated in the following account in the journal *Copeia* in March of 1967 by Mr. J. Maurice Jauffret, an experienced fisherman and observer of St. Louis, Mauritius:

" As you are aware, the whale shark is very common in our waters, and, whilst fishing, I have had many occasion to take my boat very close to them. They had showed no particular interest in the boat. Since last year, however, three fishing boats (cabin cruisers) belonging to members of our club have been attacked by three sharks whilst members of the crew were playing fish. . . . The last attack was made on my boat in which my son, Maurice, aged twenty-three, was fishing. He reported that he saw the shark near a shoal of tunny, and whilst one of his friends was bringing in a 30-pound fish, the monster (about 50 feet long) raised his head out of the water and came straight for the boat. He hit the boat astern and turned her around. The shock was so hard that all the crew were thrown down. My son then put the engine in full throttle and the shark did not follow. "

Great Blue Shark (prionace glauca)

The Blue Shark is a slender oceanic species that occurs in great abundance in warm and temperate waters throughout the world ocean. It is a familiar sight to seafarers and to offshore fishermen but seldom appears near land. The scientific names refer to its teeth, "saw-edged" (*Prionace*), and to its color, "blue-gray" (*glauca*). Formally called the Great Blue Shark, it is of the family *Carcharhinidae*, the Requiem Sharks.

Portrait of a Blue shark.

In color, the Blue Shark is blue above and white, often snow-white, underneath. The fin tips are a darker shade of blue. The body is slender and streamlined.

The pectoral fins of the Blue Shark are extremely long, saber-shaped, and supple. The other fins are modest. The tail is large, powerful, and asymmetrical, the upper lobe being much elongated. Blues have a snakelike swimming style, each muscular undulation followed by a wide fast swing of the tail. For short intervals, Blue Sharks can "sprint" at 40 to 45 miles per hour, and for longer periods they are able to sustain a speed of 25 miles per hour.

The snout is long and pointed and the mouth set well back. The eyes are large. The jaws are large, and protrusible. Blues are well armed, particularly in the upper jaw where the teeth are so crowded they overlap. The upper teeth are triangular, serrated, and sharp-edged, with tips curved out. The lower teeth are slimmer, more erect, and have finer serrations. Several rows of duplicate teeth back up the functional front rows.

Blue Sharks may grow to 15 feet or more in length but the largest recorded length is 12½ feet. They are so slimly built that a 9-footer weighs only about 150 pounds. The world's rod-and-reel record size is 11½ feet and 410 pounds, but most that are caught by anglers range from 5 to 8 feet. About 1½ feet long at birth, Blue Sharks grow to 3 feet in the first year.

Female Blue Sharks mature at age seven or eight. There is no regular breeding season; gravid females are found in all seas at all times of the year. The male fertilizes the female internally with the claspers. The gestation period is one year. The females appear to separate widely from the males to bear their young, possibly to protect them from cannibalism. The pups are born live; litters run as high as sixty or seventy. Some reports suggest that, for protection against predators, the young remain with the mother for several months, swimming in a flock around her head and body.

Blue Sharks feed at the surface of the ocean in large packs. They hunt down a wide variety of fishes such as mackerel, herring, flying fish, dogfish, cod, and pollock. They also prey on squid, capture sea birds, scavenge ship's garbage, and feast on dead or disabled whales.

Blue Sharks range throughout the warm offshore waters of the world ocean, in both the southern and northern hemisphere. In the Atlantic, Blues inhabit offshore waters from southern Canada to Uruguay on the western side, and from the North Sea to the Mediterranean and south along the African coast on the eastern side. In the eastern Pacific, they are found from southern British Columbia to Baja California. They also inhabit the offshore waters of the oceanic islands in both the Pacific and the Atlantic, and haunt the warm waters of many of the great oceanic currents like the Gulf Stream. They are perhaps the most abundant of the large oceanic sharks, often occurring in packs of hundreds.

Blue Sharks are of little interest to commercial fishermen, but deep-sea anglers fish for them occasionally. The species is considered dangerous to man, and is the suspected culprit in a number of reported attacks on swimmers and divers, though positively identified in only one or two. One would suspect that Blue Sharks were involved in many massacres of air and sea disaster castaways.

ACK

f every five persons attacked by sharks today, only one is killed. This high rate of survival is partly the result of effective rescue action and medical care. Numerous factors increase the probability of survival, including the individual shark's behavior, the defensive tactics of the victim, and the physical characteristics of the locale. In general, divers who are submerged at the time of attack fare best, and bathers who are swimming offshore at the surface fare worst. It is encouraging that the present rate of survival following shark attack is double what it was in the 1940s. Survival rates for 1,150 shark attacks summarized in Table I include only those for which data on survival is available from the U.S. Navy Shark Attack File.

The statistics in Table I were produced by my colleague H. David Baldridge, under the sponsorship of the U.S. Navy's Office of Naval Research. They were compiled from the official worldwide Shark Attack File which is now kept at the Mote Marine Laboratory in Sarasota, Florida, the base of operations at one time or another for Perry Gilbert, Stewart Springer, Eugenie Clark, and other renowned shark experts. Baldridge accumulated background data on 1,652 shark attacks. The quality of information varies greatly from case to case, but generally has improved since the Shark Research Panel was formed in 1958 by thirty-five scientists under the leadership of Dr. Gilbert.

The Shark Attack File includes all reported attacks on civilians and military personnel throughout the world ocean, though the best input is from the advanced countries, particularly the English-speaking ones. Baldridge reduced the number of cases to 1,165, all of which had enough supporting data to permit detailed analysis. About 63 percent of the attacks occurred from 1941 to 1968. To get to the leading issue in the analysis—direct attack by sharks on human beings in or on the water—he eliminated 168 cases of attacks on boats and 105 on castaways of sea disasters. Fatal cases are represented in far greater proportion than nonfatal, hospital cases more than nonhospital.

My information for the rest of this chapter is largely drawn from Baldridge's analysis of the Shark Attack File as it appears in his October 1973 report to the Office of Naval Research, *Shark Attack Against Man,* later published as *Contributions From the Mote Marine Laboratory*. Most of the tables and charts in this chapter are based on that research. An excellent summary of the results is available in Baldridge's recent book, *Shark Attack* (Berkeley Medallion Publishers), the only available case-by-case analysis done with the background information gleaned from the Navy-sponsored study. The appropriate case numbers identify the incidents of shark attack that appear from that book.

Table I:
Outcome of 1150 Shark Attacks

	NUMBER OF CASES	PERCENTAGES OF CASES
Nonfatal	744	65
Fatal, body or parts thereof recovered, death considered direct result of shark-inflicted wounds	251	22
Fatal, no details reported	70	6
Assumed fatal, body not recovered; personal gear recovered in four cases	49	4
Fatal, body or parts thereof recovered, not known if death was direct result of shark-inflicted wounds	21	2
Fatal, body or parts thereof recovered, death not considered direct result of shark-inflicted wounds	15	1

(BALDRIDGE, CONTRIBUTIONS FROM THE MOTE MARINE LABORATORY)

In the waters off Dangerous Reef, this Great White went into a frenzy as it attacked the horsemeat angled outside the cage, frightening author Peter Benchley and his cameraman.

Attack Time

Most shark attacks occur during the daylight hours. Simple logic would assume that people are more likely to be attacked in daytime because they prefer to swim or dive in well-lighted waters, and, in fact, the pattern of attack follows closely the average beach visitor's daily schedule. Attacks build up briefly in the morning, slack off at lunchtime, and then pick up to reach a peak between three and four o'clock in the afternoon. In the worldwide records, 92 percent of all shark attacks occurred in daylight, 5 percent at dawn and dusk, and 3 percent at night.

This last figure—3 percent of attacks at night—is worth considering. Night swimming certainly makes up far less than 3 percent of the general public's swimming activity. If one supposes that it is 0.3 percent, or even less, then the incidence of *attack per swimmer* would be at least ten times higher at night than in daytime. A web of circumstantial evidence, as well as the consensus of expert opinion, confirms that such a conclusion is reasonable.

Commercial fishermen know that sharks feed more actively between dusk and dawn because trial-and-error fishing has shown that the best catches are to be made in night sets. Also, shark anglers who fish from the beach learn quickly that fishing is better during nighttime hours, not only because big sharks are more active at night, but also because they come closer to the beaches then. These catch rates support the conclusion that sharks find it advantageous to feed at night when their acute sense of smell and ability to detect and zero in on moving objects gives them a clear advantage over most of their prey.

So, all the evidence now available suggests that the reason for the higher attack incidence at night is the nocturnal feeding habits of most of the dangerous shark species. In my own underwater rambles, I have observed that sharks tend to move up from deep water at dusk to search coral reefs and other shallow places along the coast for food. My one close brush with a large Hammerhead Shark occurred at Looe Key, Florida, at 5:30 P.M. one April evening.

Attack Depth and Place

One would expect the greatest number of shark attacks where the greatest crowds of people gather to swim. Not only do the records confirm this, but they also

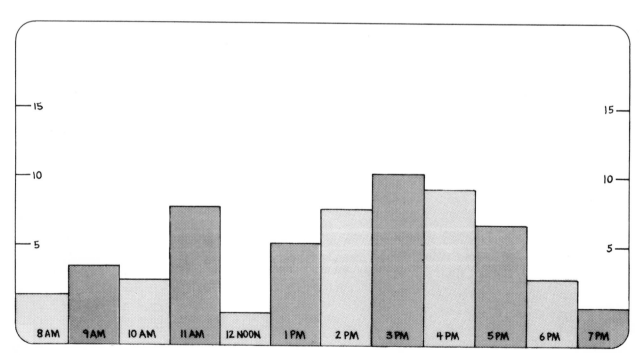

FIG. 1. WORLDWIDE U.S. NAVY RECORDS SHOW THAT SHARK ATTACKS BUILD UP THROUGH THE MORNING HOURS, SLACK OFF AT LUNCHTIME, THEN REACH A PEAK IN MIDAFTERNOON. (SOURCE: BALDRIDGE, *CONTRIBUTIONS FROM THE MOTE MARINE LABORATORY*)

show that the majority of attacks take place in wading depths, where most people spend most of their time in the water. Baldridge shows the following depths for 470 victims:

WATER DEPTH	NUMBER OF ATTACKS
0–5 feet	290
6–20 feet	110
21–50 feet	51
51 feet and deeper	19

It would be overhasty to conclude from the above statistics that shallow waters are the most dangerous just because the 290 wading-depth attacks represent 62 percent of the total. Logic suggests the opposite. The remaining 38 percent of attacks is more significant because the average bather spends far less than 38 percent of his time in deeper water. It is likely that a smaller percent of swimming takes place in deeper water. If this supposition is reasonable, the fact that 38 percent of the attacks take place where only 4 percent of the activity occurs suggests that the risk of shark attacks is far greater in water deeper than 5 feet.

The distance from shore where attacks occur seems to correlate more highly with the concentration and availability of victims than with shark behavior as we know it. Few bathers are attacked offshore because few bathers venture far from the beach. At the typical resort beach, by far the majority of bathers are found within 100 feet of shore, with only a very small percentage out beyond 200 feet. Yet about 34 percent of 279 attacks that involved beach activities took place more than 200 feet from shore. The obvious conclusion is that there is a very real increase in the risk of shark attack as a bather moves out from shore.

Shark species that have the worst reputations for attacking man are those that inhabit the coastal regions and follow their prey into the shallows. Attacks by these species have occurred in such shallow water that the charging shark has actually beached itself in its eagerness to reach its victim.

It is revealing to examine the depth to which the individual was submerged when attacked. Baldridge

shows the following depths of the victims in 881 analyzed attacks:

VICTIM DEPTH	NUMBER OF ATTACKS
0–5 feet	797
6–20 feet	59
21–50 feet	22
50 feet and deeper	12

Here again, a careful interpretation of the data is necessary. A superficial conclusion would be that the probability of attack is less in subsurface waters, but the contrary is almost certainly true. Note that 10 percent of attack victims were totally submerged—that is, deeper than 6 feet. Now, it is very unlikely that 10 percent of the people in the water at beaches or off-shore are routinely to be found submerged 6 feet or more below the surface. Normally, only divers would go this deep. Compared to the great mass of bathers throughout the world, divers constitute only a very small percentage of persons exposed to shark attack, certainly less than 10 percent and probably much less than 1 percent. If, therefore, 10 percent of shark attacks are on this very small percent of submerged persons, the inevitable conclusion is that divers expose themselves to a very high risk of attack. Of course, part of the explanation is that divers generally move farther out than ordinary surface swimmers to gain depth, and as previously discussed, to move farther offshore is to make encounter with a shark more likely. All in all, the risk of attack would appear to be much higher for submerged divers than for surface swimmers.

The deepest attack on record occurred at 230 feet in Cane Bay, St. Croix, on October 1972. Rodney Temple and his diving partner were preparing to ascend to the surface when two White-Tipped Sharks charged them, forcing the men to flee in search of a safe retreat. In the panic, the two were separated. According to Temple's partner:

" I looked down and couldn't believe the turbulence and silt that was clouding the bottom below me. Temple's air bubbles were coming out of the turbulence and he was apparently moving deeper. I swam down the line of bubbles. Visibility in the murky water was about 3 feet and I bumped into him before I saw him. I put one arm on his harness and tried to pull us up the bank. I was aware of him screaming into his mouthpiece and alternate violent shocks and tugs at his legs. We were both being pulled deeper in what I assumed was a shark attack. His body was sustaining violent shocks, and twisting at irregular intervals. We were turned over after one, and it was then that I ran completely out of air. I held my breath and tried to turn to face Temple. I gave him signals indicating that I was out of air. He gave no sign of recognition. I attempted to reach across his chest to the secondary air supply he was carrying and could not reach it as we were upset again. I estimate that I had held my breath over a minute at that point. I realized that I was slowly blacking out and pulled his safety vest and dropped his weight belt. I gave one last pull and felt him torn away. I can remember thinking that he was already dead before the last attack pulled him away. He was apparently lifeless, limp, and the screaming had stopped. He quite probably had exhausted his primary air supply and was unable to negotiate the switch to his alternate. At this point, he would mercifully have succumbed to unconsciousness due to anoxia. My gauge was reading 270 feet when I reached him several minutes before. I had no idea of our present depth; approximately 300 feet. I pulled my safety vest, put my head back, exhaling and started for the surface.

The partner was not struck by the sharks but suffered permanent lung damage from his rapid ascent. No part of Temple was ever recovered. (C #1656)

Though the *rate* of attack on people in deep water is higher, still the locale of most attacks is near shore where the preponderance of bathers are found. In other words, sharks have attacked divers and victims of sea disasters at a higher rate of frequency in deep water, though they have claimed more overall victims along shorelines where more shark encounters are likely to occur. Consider the following breakdown of types of habitat for 948 analyzed attacks:

Beaches and shore areas in general	435
Sandbars, reefs, and banks	179
Rivers and river mouths	95
Harbors and bays	89
Open sea	88
Near breakwaters, piers, and jetties	41
Outside breaker/surf line	21

(BALDRIDGE, CONTRIBUTIONS FROM THE MOTE MARINE LABORATORY)

It is significant that 19 percent of the attacks occurred in the vicinity of sea-bottom features such as sandbars and coral reefs where there is relatively shallow water close to channels, troughs, or other deep waters where sharks can lurk in the comfort of dark and safe waters. The fate of Norman Girvan is a grim example. At Kirra Beach, Australia, in New South Wales, on October 27, 1937, Girvan, Jack Brinkley, and a companion were swimming over a sandbar about 100 yards from shore when Girvan screamed, "Quick, a shark's got me." From the bloodied water he extended his hand to the companion, who later said:

I tried to take him by the arm and found that it was just hanging by a bit of flesh. Brinkley turned to swim towards us and just then he began to kick and struggle as though he also had been attacked. Girvan said, "It won't let go, it's got my leg." I felt Girvan being shaken forcibly, and he was pulled out of my arms. I felt the body of a shark brush my thigh. Girvan said, "I'm gone—goodbye."

At that moment Girvan slid under the water and never rose again. The attacker, a 12-foot Tiger Shark that was caught the following day, had Girvan's arms and legs in its stomach. (C #37)

The evidence suggests that the risk of shark attack is highest around sea bottoms that rise up next to deeper channels offering easy ingress from the sea. The attack on thirteen-year-old Michael Land at Winklespruit, South Africa, is a case in point. At 7:35

P.M. on January 6, 1969, Land's school vacation turned to disaster. The boy was standing on a submerged rock in murky water 2 to 3 feet deep, approximately 60 feet offshore, when something rough and heavy scraped his foot. He reached down to check the problem only to have his right hand slashed. Screaming, he attracted two lifesavers, who arrived as the stricken boy collapsed into the water. As his rescuers carried him ashore, a vicious Bull Shark (locally called a Zambezi), 6 to 7 feet long, emerged and tracked them all the way in. Land survived but his right foot was completely severed.

Another locale involved in many brutal attacks is the lagoon that is so typically formed along sandy beaches inside an outer bar. This may be a risky place at high tide when a large shark can easily move over the outer bar and into the lagoon. This danger is illustrated by the case of sixteen-year-old David Vogensen who was enjoying a summer outing with a friend on the California coast north of Bodega Head on August 20, 1975. Leaving his friend on a sandbar about 60 yards offshore, Vogensen swam toward the surf zone and was lazily breaststroking in the lagoon while waiting to catch a wave. Suddenly, a huge fin emerged and raced toward him. Vogensen screamed and beat the water to frighten the monster off. He felt no pain, no pull, but his left foot went dead. As he stumbled from the water, his trunks ripped away and he could see he was badly wounded in the groin. His left foot, upper thighs, and lower abdomen were badly lacerated as well, but he had survived the attack. The culprit was identified as a White Shark, 12 to 14 feet long, that had entered the lagoon over a low place in the sandbar.

Geography of Attack

Since sharks occur throughout the world ocean except in the Antarctic Sea, the potential hazard of attack is nearly oceanwide. Sharks attack man whenever the two meet—in the open sea, in bays, harbors, inlets, tidal rivers, and even in a few freshwater lakes.

The most hazardous part of the sea is the east coast of Australia. Shark attacks along this coast—from Torres Strait in the North to Melbourne in the south —account for more than one-third of all recorded attacks.

The next most dangerous part of the sea appears to be the Atlantic coast of the United States, which accounts for 20 percent of the 1,165 attacks in the U.S. Navy's Shark Attack File. States with over 10 recorded attacks include New Jersey (17), South Carolina (23), California (46), and Florida (107). The high incidence of attack in California and Florida is related to the popularity of two dangerous sports in these states —diving and spearfishing. The cool coastal waters of California are favorite haunts of the Great White Shark, or Maneater, while the warm waters of Florida are attractive to a host of dangerous sharks.

The third highest incidence occurs off the South African coast—about 10 percent of worldwide attacks happen here. The scourge of this coast is the Bull Shark, which mysteriously arrives each year in December and remains through April.

Why should there be such high rates of attack off Australia, South Africa, and the United States? Common sense suggests, first, because a high proportion of people in these countries swim and dive. Second, since they are all English-speaking countries, the flow of communication between them is highly developed. It has been more difficult for the Navy project to obtain reports from non-English–speaking nations, especially from the less developed countries.

Although sharks populate much of the world ocean, most attacks have occurred within a 5,200-mile-band zone centered on the equator and extending around the world. This shark hazard zone, delineated by the Australian expert V. M. Coppelson, extends from around 40° NL to about 40° SL. Within this broad zone there is a 2,800-mile band, centered on the equator, that extends south to the Tropic of Capricorn and north to the Tropic of Cancer. Here the shark hazard exists year-round. There are also two 1,200-mile bands extending to the north (Cancer to 40° NL) and south (Capricorn to 40° SL) that become hazardous seasonally. Each band extends the full 1,200 miles poleward from the tropics during the peak of summer: July and August in the northern hemisphere, and January and February in the southern hemisphere. Coppelson sees the shark hazard as limited to a 4,000-mile-wide band that alternately shifts north and south across the tropics with the seasons.

All available reports indicate that attacks outside

of the zone from 40° NL to 40° SL are few, and that they almost never occur above 47° NL or below 46° SL. Not only are sharks less abundant in the higher latitudes, but the colder waters there also discourage swimming and diving. There is a much higher proportion of attacks on boats than on persons in the waters north of 40° NL.

Table II: Localities of 1153 Worldwide Shark Attacks for Which Data on Locale Were Available	
Australia, New Zealand, and New Guinea	401
United States	225
Pacific Ocean, islands	137
Africa (principally South Africa)	117
Asia	83
West Indies	55
Central America	47
Open sea	32
Mediterranean Sea	30
Atlantic Ocean, islands	7
South America	6
Persian Gulf	6
Indian Ocean, islands	4
England	3
Red Sea	2

(BALDRIDGE, CONTRIBUTIONS FROM THE MOTE MARINE LABORATORY)

Table III: Localities of 223 U.S. Shark Attacks for Which Data on Locale Were Available	
Massachusetts	4
Connecticut	1
New York	3
New Jersey	17
Delaware	2
Virginia	2
North Carolina	2
South Carolina	23
Georgia	6
Florida, East Coast	61
Florida Keys	17
Florida, West Coast	27
(Florida, area unknown)	2
Mississippi	1
Texas	2
California, northern	20
California, southern	26

(BALDRIDGE, CONTRIBUTIONS FROM THE MOTE MARINE LABORATORY)

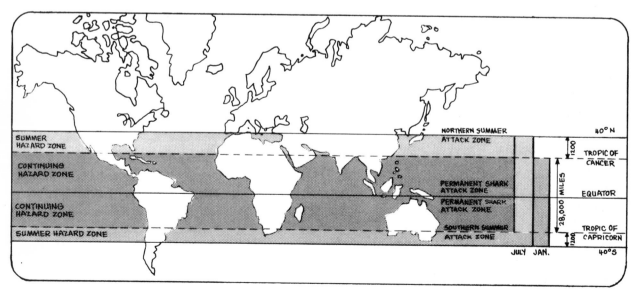

FIG. 3. SEASONAL SHARK HAZARD ZONES.

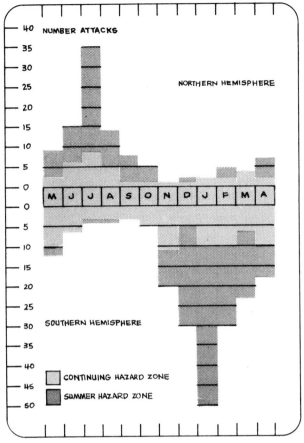

FIG. 2. MONTHLY INCIDENCE OF SHARK ATTACKS IN THE NORTHERN AND SOUTHERN HEMISPHERES.

The victim of the most northerly shark attack in waters off the Atlantic Coast of the United States was a sixteen-year-old boy, Joseph Troy, Jr. He and an older male companion were swimming 10 feet apart and 150 yards from the beach in Buzzards Bay, Massachusetts, when a Great White Shark suddenly gripped his left leg and pulled him under. Troy fought the shark underwater, finally breaking its grip. His companion then held him afloat while the shark prowled the blood-stained scene, stalking the luckless swimmers. Before the shark could strike again, a rescue boat arrived. However, the wounds proved fatal and Troy died in the hospital during amputation of his grossly mutilated leg.

The most southerly attacks occur off the coast of New Zealand, where temperatures may be in the fifties. On September 15, 1968, in the chilly 55° F. water of Otago Harbor, a 14-foot Great White Shark ravaged Graham Hitt. According to an eyewitness account, the

shark with an eye "as large as a baseball," balanced and pivoted on its pectoral fins in a strange manner, positioned itself, then veered and made directly for Hitt. The twenty-four-year-old spearfisherman was clad in a black wetsuit and was swimming at the surface. The shark struck in a vortex of churning water, seized Hitt's left leg, shook him, and suddenly let him go. It circled once and then left as quickly as it had come. In spite of a prompt rescue by members of his five-man spearfishing team, the single bite was enough to sever Hitt's femoral artery, killing the diver before he even reached shore.

In the three countries with the most incidents (South Africa, Australia, and the United States), there are more attacks along the eastern than the western

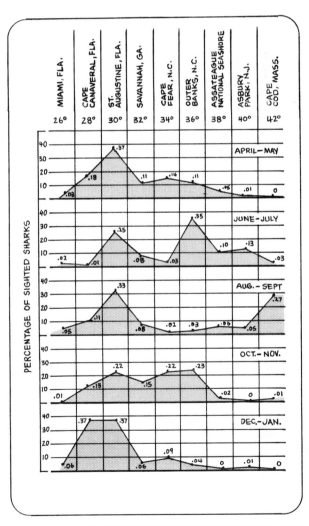

FIG. 5. THE NATURAL SEASONAL MIGRATIONS OF SHARKS ALONG THE U.S. ATLANTIC COAST BRING THEM NORTH FOR THE SUMMER BEACH SEASON. (DATA FROM U.S. COAST GUARD OCEANOGRAPHIC UNIT, JULY 1969–JULY 1973.)

coast. In Australia and South Africa, about ten times as many attacks occur along the eastern coasts, while in the United States, there are four times as many there. This higher incidence correlates with the warm currents that extend up the eastern coasts of these countries, attracting both sharks and swimmers to the same locale.

Shark attacks are quite rare near the equator. They reach their peak in the centers of both summer hazard zones, which suggests that the temperature in the equatorial zone is too warm for most sharks. But it is difficult to generalize on the temperature preferences of sharks because these differ from species to species. The White Shark, or Maneater, for example,

FIG. 4. MAJOR OCEAN CURRENTS OF THE WORLD. WARM CURRENTS ARE SHOWN BY SOLID LINES, COLD CURRENTS BY BROKEN LINES. (MILLER, ROBERT C., THE SEA, RANDOM HOUSE, 1966)

likes a colder environment and is abundant where water temperatures are in the sixties. The Mako Shark, on the other hand, is abundant only in waters of 70° F. and higher, while the Tiger Shark occurs rarely in waters below 70° F. and the Porbeagle, a cousin of the Mako, inhabits waters below 65° F. Most of the dangerous species do prefer waters 68° F. or higher, however, and unfortunately their preference coincides with that of most bathers. This is the root of the shark menace. The official records show that 75 percent of attacks by all species of sharks throughout the world occurred in temperatures in the range of 70° to 85° F. Of the 196 analyzed attacks, 89 occurred in waters from 70° F. to 75° F., 67 in waters warmer than 78° F., and only 39 in all waters colder than 68° F.

In the United States, the mass of sharks (89 percent) observed in winter are found below 30° NL, from Jacksonville south along the Florida coast, according to records compiled by the U.S. Coast Guard Oceanographic Unit from monthly aerial surveys during the period July 1969–June 1974. In the spring, they begin to appear farther north, until by June and July, 63 percent are sighted between Cape Hatteras and southern New Jersey. August and September, the warmest months, bring 15 percent of the Hammerheads and 30 percent of all other sharks to the area stretching from northern New Jersey to Cape Cod. In the early autumn, the sharks move south until, by the end of November, they are again concentrated in Florida. Florida is unique in that it has a continuing shark hazard—even in summer, the sightings never drop below 38 percent of the coastal total. During the winter months, Florida has 85 to 90 percent of the sighted sharks.

In addition to regular seasonal migrations, sharks often move in response to short-term changes in the environment. This can increase the hazard of attack. For example, on the U.S. Pacific coast, unusually warm water was alleged to have contributed to the attack on sixteen-year-old Suzanne Theriot on May 19, 1960. The girl was floating on an inner tube in the company of three school friends off the beach at Monterey Bay when a foot-high dorsal fin circled the group. The shark struck hard once with its jaws, twisting and tearing her leg. Her friends loaded her onto the inner tube and kicked furiously shoreward. A tourniquet was quickly applied, and although her leg was amputated, she survived. Newspaper accounts of the story blamed

the attack on "warming of the waters and the movement of warm-water fish northward." (C #686)

One major exception to the warm-water rule is the White Shark, which may attack in temperatures anywhere between 50° and 80° F., though 78 percent of its recorded attacks have been in waters lower than 70° F. Most attacks in the cool ocean waters off the California coast are by White Sharks.

Shark Attacks

The shark that strikes is typically 7 feet long and weighs 200 pounds. It has a jaw 1 foot across and teeth an inch long. These dimensions are based on averages for the dangerous species.

Obviously if one sees an attacking shark coming, one's chances of survival are improved. But prior sighting has occurred in only 37 percent of the attacks in analyzed official records. Therefore, it is more likely that a shark will strike unseen.

Only rarely will a shark be observed circling its victim. Official case records show that in 161 attacks where the shark was clearly observed, it made straightway approaches to the victims in 66 cases (41 percent), passing close to or glancing off other persons in the water before striking the victim in 20 of those attacks. In 34 cases (21 percent) the sharks circled the victims prior to attacking.

Attacks in 15 cases (9 percent) followed soon after the sighting of a shark between the victim and some barrier or obstacle such as the beach, a reef, or a boat. A shark threatened by having its escape to the open sea cut off by the presence of a human in the water is a potentially aggressive, dangerous animal.

When the shark is seen, there is about an even chance that it is already bearing down upon its victim, perhaps so intent on its objective that it ignores all other persons nearby, though it may brush close to them as it presses the attack on its selected prey. This singleness of purpose is well demonstrated in the case of seventeen-year-old Barry Wilson.

Just after being warned by a skin diver that the bleeding wounds on his body caused by surfing could attack a shark, Wilson plunged into the cool, murky water 75 feet off Point Aulone, California, on December 7, 1952. A spectator watching from the rocky

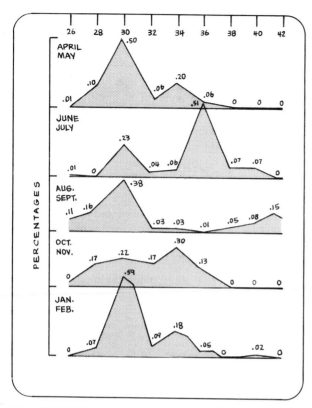

FIG. 6. PERCENTAGE DISTRIBUTION OF U.S. SHARK SIGHTINGS (EXCLUDING HAMMERHEADS), JULY 1969–JULY 1974. (DATA FROM U.S. COAST GUARD OCEANOGRAPHIC UNIT.)

point saw Wilson suddenly jerk erect in the water. Immediately, a large shark surfaced and, methodically aiming its 12-foot bulk straight at the boy, struck from the front, thrusting Wilson's whole torso clear of the water. The spectator saw Wilson, draped over the shark's back, fighting desperately with both hands to free himself. He then shot upward, emerging at the surface in a pool of blood. The shark made two more passes at the victim, disappeared, then resurfaced and hit Wilson again, just as five rescuers were attempting to slide him onto a rubber tube. All the way through heavy surf to the beach the monster tracked the victim, glancing and scraping against the rescuers but never striking them with its jaws. Wilson died from the massive loss of flesh and blood from separate strikes on four parts of his body—back and left leg (from the first hit), inner right thigh (from the following strike), upper left leg (while he fought), and right thigh (during rescue). (C #236)

I share with several colleagues the belief that the shark hazard is greater in murky waters. I believe this for two reasons. First, a shark can far more easily mistake human for natural prey in the murkiness, or blunder into an aggressive attack because of its poor daytime eyesight. Second, the person under attack in murky waters has less of a chance of seeing the attacker coming, and thus of evading or defending against it, particularly if he is submerged at the time.

The murkiness of the water off Cypress Point, California, on January 23, 1966, undoubtedly set up skin diver Don Barthman for attack:

" My face was in the water, but I didn't see the shark coming. The sea was a little murky—he came up on the side out of nowhere. He hit like a freight train . . . cracked a rib and left four teeth marks on my chest. He seemed to shove me through the water . . . jaws closed on my left arm. He shook me around in the water like a puppy dog . . . ripped a 5-inch gash, almost to the bone . . . and swam off for another attack. As he came in the second time . . . I put out my left hand to protect myself and it went right into his mouth . . . his teeth ripped along the crease . . . and cut the tendon. He went away again, and the water was now murky enough so I couldn't see him anywhere. That really worried me. I thought he'd come up at the rear and grab my legs. I yelled for help, 'Shark! Shark!' They pulled me into a boat. . . . " (C #1398)

FIG. 9. WORLDWIDE FREQUENCY OF SHARK ATTACK IN WATERS OF VARIOUS TEMPERATURES. (BALDRIDGE, *CONTRIBUTIONS FROM THE MOTE MARINE LABORATORY*)

Once an attacking shark selects a victim, it persists tenaciously. In 23 percent of the official cases, the shark held fast to its victim with its jaws even during rescue operations. In two-thirds of these cases, the jaws had to be forced open to effect the release of the victim. When Dr. H. Warmke speared a 5-foot Nurse Shark on August 12, 1954, the fish rolled and tangled

MEAN NUMBER OF HAMMERHEAD SHARKS CAUGHT PER MONTH

SPRING   SUMMER   AUTUMN   WINTER
PERIOD 1953—61

FIG. 8. SEASONAL VARIATION IN ABUNDANCE OF HAMMERHEADS OFF DURBAN (DAVIES, DAVID H., *ABOUT SHARKS AND SHARK ATTACK,* SHUTER AND SHOOTER, PIETERMARITZ, SOUTH AFRICA, 1964)

him in the cable of his spear. Even after another man, Dr. Teas, also speared the shark, its attention remained fixed on Warmke. It struck him twice on the right leg and once on the left, tearing off flesh. Finally Teas tried to grab the shark by the tail, but it twisted around and clamped so firmly onto his right knee that no efforts to pry open the jaws succeeded. Only after an energetic knife attack killed the shark were the two men able to force the jaws open and get Teas released. (C #717)

Of the various modes of attack, one stands out as extraordinarily horrible. It is called *frenzy,* a maniacal condition of sharks so excited with violence that they attack with fury all that comes within range of their jaws. Induced by the smells and sights of abundant prey, the frenzy builds gradually to an orgy of feeding that climaxes only after the attackers vent their fury and sink exhausted to the depths from which they rose. An occasional bout of frenzy is a natural part of shark behavior, with the energy of the event aimed at high-efficiency feeding on fish schools or other typical prey. But against man, this famous frenzy appears to be aimed at satisfying drives other than hunger.

Frenzy attacks usually inflict multiple bites and massive wounds on the victim. Of 675 cases where the number of bites was recorded, 74 percent of the victims were bitten only once or twice. In 18 percent of the cases, victims suffered from 3 to 5 wounds. Repeated strikes, resulting in gross multiple wounds, occurred in 8 percent of the recorded cases. To state the obvious, frenzy attacks result in multiple lacerations and gross mutilation.

As one might expect, the victims of a frenzy attack do not fare well. Official records show that 63 percent die, which is nearly twice the average rate of 35 percent for all shark victims. The victim's body, or at least part of it, is usually recovered after a frenzy attack. In only six of forty-nine official frenzy cases had the body completely disappeared. The case of scuba diver William Dandridge is typical. Dandridge and two friends anchored their boat on a coral patch near Key Biscayne, Florida, on June 24, 1961, to dive and spear some fish. Ten minutes later, Dandridge surfaced abruptly screaming, "Help! I need help!", then slid back under the water. After two days of searching, his body was found within the corals of the reef about 20 feet away from his loaded spear gun. The right arm

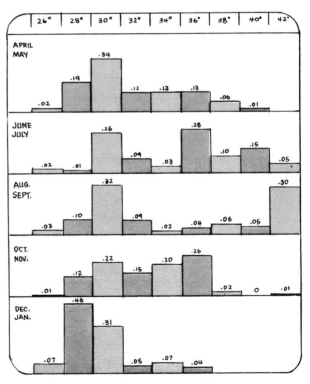

FIG. 7. PERCENTAGE DISTRIBUTION OF HAMMERHEAD SHARKS, U.S. SHARK SIGHTINGS, JULY 1969–JULY 1973. (DATA FROM U.S. COAST GUARD OCEANOGRAPHIC UNIT.)

Only the air tanks of diver John Rochette are visible as a twenty-five-foot maneater tears at his leg (water froth, left) while fellow diver Jack Bolger tries to help.

and entire left side were gone and the rest was badly raked by the teeth of the attacking shark, whose species is still unknown. (C #899)

On the other hand, awesome cases of complete disappearance are listed in the official records. James Neal was a member of a six-man scuba diving party observing sea life at a depth of 80 feet along a reef about 8 miles off Panama City, Florida, on August 15, 1959. On the return trip to the boat, Neal vanished. The party's guide crew searched in vain for him. Checking with others in the area, they heard reports from fishermen that sharks were around. A U.S. Navy diver who joined the search was confronted by a 12-foot Blue Shark and darted to safety in a reef as a large Mako Shark appeared to join the Blue Shark in several threatening passes "as close as six inches to my face." He escaped during a lull in the performance, surfaced, and made it to his boat. On the following day, a team of Navy divers recovered pieces of clothing and equipment, ripped and scattered over a 100-square-foot area: torn flippers, a mask, weights, a belt in shreds, a spear gun, a knife with its leather sheath, and torn bits of undershirt and swimming trunks. Though neither the body nor the double scuba tanks of Neal were ever found, it was assumed he had been attacked and killed by a shark. (C #439)

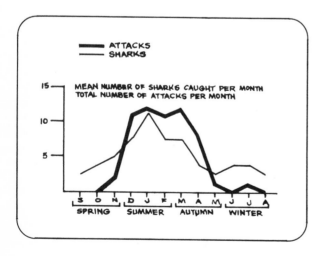

In order to achieve more dramatic results, many underwater photographers will tease sharks into a dangerous state of frenzy. Here, a Great White snaps at a sack of horsemeat for the cameras of Ron and Valerie Taylor (right).

Mutilation of Victims

The official case records show that 74 percent of initial contacts were sudden and violent regardless of the direction from which the attacker came. In 296 cases where the direction of strike was known, the percentage breakdown was as follows:

From front of victim	33 percent
From rear of victim	31 percent
From side of victim	17 percent
From below the victim	16 percent
From above the victim	3 percent

(BALDRIDGE, CONTRIBUTIONS FROM THE MOTE MARINE LABORATORY)

Appendages are the favored object of attack, as shown in 835 official cases. Wounds to arms, hands, legs, and feet account for 78 percent of all wounds. It is not surprising that legs are the most often damaged part of the body when we recall that 62 percent of attacks at beaches have occurred in water waist deep or less. Also, victims use their hands, fingers, and arms to ward off attack, so these parts of the body are often torn off or mangled. Wounds to the head were rarely reported—the bodies of some victims have been skeletonized and yet the head has remained relatively untouched—though in a few attacks, victims have been decapitated by sharks.

The following body parts were involved in 1482 citations:

BODY PART	NUMBER OF INJURIES
Calf and knee	334
Thigh	271
Arms	193
Feet	146
Hands	126
Buttocks	88
Abdomen and stomach	84
Fingers and toes	63
Chest	46
Waist	30
Back	32
Shoulder	31
Head	18
Genitals	20

(BALDRIDGE, CONTRIBUTIONS FROM THE MOTE MARINE LABORATORY)

In shark attack cases where clean-cut, gash-type wounds are left in a single line, it is usually not possible to ascertain which jaw was involved—the upper or the lower. However, because of the better arrangement of the upper teeth (flat, broad, sharply pointed, with serrated edges) for the purpose of cutting, they are more likely to be involved in producing gash-type wounds.

The primary cause of death associated with shark attack is loss of blood from massive wounds, and shock, complicated by drowning. Most victims survive if treated promptly and skillfully.

The body cavities of victims were fatally slashed open in only 5 percent of the official cases; the trunk was severed in only 1 percent; virtually total removal of flesh from the victim's skeleton occurred in another 1 percent; and the whole victim was swallowed in a final 1 percent. (See Table IV.)

Table IV: The Percentage of Analyzed Shark Attack Victims Who Received Each of 10 Different Types of Wounds

Wound Description	Percentage of Victims Receiving Wound	Number of Cases Considered
Severe lacerations/displacement of tissue	78	765
Lacerations, no significant loss or displacement of tissue	71	501
Significant loss of tissue	55	721
Bone exposed	46	646
Bites, discontinuous tooth marks, etc.	42	397
Scrapes, abrasions	23	513
Appendage lost to shark	19	876
Appendage lost through surgery	7	936
Body cavity opened	5	833
Trunk severed by shark	1	959
Body skeletonized or swallowed whole	1	978

(BALDRIDGE, CONTRIBUTIONS FROM THE MOTE MARINE LABORATORY)

One is curious about divers as a group because they contrast a high risk of attack against a low rate of fatality, particularly when submerged. The incidence of injury to the upper bodies of submerged divers is about equal to that for bathers and other victims, but damage to the lower regions occurs far less often. This illustrates the general proposition that divers fare better under attack by sharks than do bathers. Divers are also more likely to receive lacerations without significant loss or displacement of flesh. Exposure of bone happened less than half as often. Bite marks were more frequent with divers, but scrapes and abrasions were less frequent, probably because of the wetsuits they wear. Loss of a limb to a shark happened only one-third as often to submerged divers as to victims in general.

Personal Factors That Invite Attack

Prior to attack, very few, if any, of the living victims of sharks were seriously wounded, and therefore bleeding profusely. Ninety-nine percent of the victims were considered to have been alive at the time of the attack. In only 2 or 3 percent of the cases were the victims bleeding to even a minor extent from coral, rock, or shell cuts, open sores, or the like prior to attack.

While routine attacks show that the overwhelming number of shark attacks are on uninjured persons, the case files of ship sinkings and airplane crashes indicate that injured persons are more liable to attack. Human blood in the water certainly does appear to attract sharks, and from great distances. Wartime stories told by the survivors of sea disasters have a common theme: castaways in life rafts are safe from attack until blood or vomit from injured or seasick persons flows into the water and incites sharks to charge the rafts.

While arguing sharks, merchant mariners tend to line up firmly on one or the other side of the issue of "dead or alive," depending on their experiences and biases. Many believe that sharks attack only corpses, while others hold that living castaways are the more attractive prey. The statistics support neither side in the argument. In some cases, sharks took only corpses, while in others, they attacked live bodies.

The sinking of the *Nova Scotia* off Natal in November 1942 is an example of live-body preference. When torpedoed by a German U-boat, the ship had 765 Italian prisoners of war and 134 South African soldiers aboard. The first explosion burned up most of the lifeboats, and secondary explosions scattered dead and dying prisoners over the water. Many were swimming with life belts and clutching to rafts and wreckage. The following morning, rescuers found that sharks had taken all of the living and were swimming unconcernedly among a mass of corpses.

But other survivors have related that the sharks they encountered were mainly scavengers of dead flesh. Unique in shark annals is the thirty-one-hour survival tale told by an Ecuadorian flight officer in George A. Llano's *Airmen Against the Sea*. With two companions, he ditched off the coast of Ecuador on a flight between Esmereldas and Salinas. The three men removed their clothing before entering the water; all had life vests. One man was hurt and bleeding freely from the nose.

All this occurred Thursday, approximately between four and five of the afternoon. Then placing myself between them so that they could take hold of the harness of my life preserver we proceeded swimming. Later night fell and the desperation and terrification of my companions was increasing progressively, as the sea in that section is very rough and the waves caused my companions to swallow water. It was there that Colonel B., at a time estimated by me some five hours after the moment of the accident, died.

Afterwards putting the corpse, which floated perfectly, in front of me, I continued pushing it, with the objective of taking it out if we managed to reach land. When I had pushed the corpse of my Colonel ahead of me in order to swim to it again, a strange force dragged the body and I did not again see it in spite of searching a long time among the waves. Sub-Lieutenant D., who was still living, and who had hold of me, made me reflect that it was foolish to wait longer and I continued toward where I believed the coast to be. Sub-Lieutenant D. lived perhaps four or five hours more until the end. After having had moments . . . of a state of despair which is very painful to narrate, he died. . . .

I put the body of my companion in front of me and continued pushing him, but not as far ahead as I had done previously with the other corpse. As it was a moonlight night, and during some moments very clear, I was able to observe that strange figures crossed very close to us, until at a given moment I felt that they were trying to take away the corpse, pulling it by the feet, on account of which I clutched desperately the body of my companion . . . until . . . I touched his legs and became aware that a part of them was lacking. . . . continued swimming with the now mutilated corpse until the attack was repeated two times more, and then, terrorized at feeling the contact of fish against my body, turned loose the corpse . . . convinced that I would be the next victim. . . . As soon as it was light, I could see the coast at a great distance, but I had no hopes of reaching it because with the light of day I could clearly see that various sharks were following me. . . . When I moved my legs slowly, with the object of resting, I touched with my feet the bodies of these animals which were constantly below mine in order to attack me. I would then thrash the water and thus for a few moments the danger would pass. I continued swimming all day Friday until at sundown I found myself some four or five hundred meters from the rock on the coast. As I was already tired . . . because of the undertow . . . I could not reach the rocks until after making a superhuman effort.

If you are male, you are thirteen times more susceptible to shark attack than if you are female. Records show that 93 percent of worldwide shark attacks are against men. One logical explanation is that women are exposed to attack far less than men because they stay closer to shore, scuba dive less often, and tend to remain with groups. In order to check this, the shark attack statisticians excluded all diving, sport fishing, and other such activities where males tend to predominate and concentrated on swimming beaches where the activity ratio of men to women should be more equal. The results were shocking—on the beaches, sharks attack men nine times oftener than women! The statisticians qualify this, however, by explaining that in their observation, males were generally more active when in the water. Is it possible that this difference in activity alone accounts for the enormous difference in rate of attack? The official explanation, inconclusive but interesting, suggests that the shark's bias may also be influenced by some different smell emanating from males.

My own attempt to answer the question statistically was a disappointment. It seemed to me that if differences in activity were the explanation, I would find that women stayed closer to shore and were therefore less vulnerable. To a small extent this was true, but the difference was far too slight to explain the nine-to-one ratio of attacks.

In six analyzed cases where females were attacked beyond 200 feet from shore, one woman was fishing while standing in waist-deep water on an offshore reef, two fell overboard from a boat, one was body surfing, and two were swimming well offshore.

In order to find a base for comparison, H. David Baldridge compiled some data from Myrtle Beach to typify bather distribution. These figures, compared to the official records of shark attack around the world, are given in Table V.

From these figures, it must be concluded that if there is a simple mechanistic reason for the high attack rate on males, it does not lie in differences in activity depth. Except for the deepest area (which has little statistical effect because so few attacks occurred there), the proportion of male to female bathers at depth intervals is no higher than 4 to 2, while attack proportions run from 11 to 2 up to 20 to 2. So, after correcting for distribution differences in bathers, attacking sharks have a preference of about five to one for male bathers.

Very little is known about the chemical interchange occurring between people and the water they are immersed in. Perhaps, to sharks, males smell different than females. It may be that there is some hormonal substance peculiar to males that sharks interpret as threatening and to which they respond with aggressive behavior. Or the female menstrual cycle may be a factor. The explanation must lie outside normal appetite because a considerable percentage of shark attacks do not appear to be motivated by hunger. There is no explanation for the disproportionate number of male victims. The official conclusion: "Clearly, there is here a need for further basic research."

Table V: Comparison of
Shark Attack Victims by Sex

	TYPICAL BATHERS			ATTACK VICTIMS		
	Male	Female	Ratio	Male	Female	Ratio
Knee deep	17	15	2:2	20	2	20:2
Knee to waist	37	26	3:2	56	10	11:2
Waist to neck	50	26	4:2	43	5	17:2
Neck to over head	18	2	9:2	5	1	10:2

(BALDRIDGE, CONTRIBUTIONS FROM THE MOTE MARINE LABORATORY)

Teenagers and young adults are the principal victims of sharks. But, of course, teenagers and young adults are highly available to sharks because they spend so much time at the beach and in the water. The median age of victims, about twenty-two years, roughly corresponds to the median age of all water users. In the words of Baldridge:

> Minimal restraint is felt in concluding that there is little in victim-age data (median as well as spread of ages about the median) to indicate that sharks select victims of any particular age grouping. Instead, victims appear to have been selected from all ages making up the population of people normally expected to be involved in recreational use of waters at or near beaches.

Whether skin color and race have any causative significance is an open question. The records show quite clearly that no race is immune from attack, but they give no hint as to sharks' racial preferences. However, skin color and contrasting areas of skin pigmentation do appear to influence shark attack, which is why divers sometimes darken the lighter palms of their hands and the soles of their feet. A recommended strategy for bathers is to protect themselves by placing the lighter palms of their hands under their armpits at the first sighting of a shark.

In at least five of the official cases, the locus of initial strike on the victims (presumably white) was an area of "uneven tanning of the skin." The analysts do not comment whether these five were among the fifty-three nude swimmers attacked (7.5 percent of all recorded incidents).

Wearing Apparel and Equipment

Shark experts have spent a lot of time studying the effects on shark attack behavior of different kinds of bathing suit and other apparel. As one might expect, it is far easier to learn what 50 to 100 victims wore while attacked in a particular year than to learn what multiple millions of bathers and divers who were not attacked were wearing. A statistically valid comparison is obviously not possible; nonetheless it is instructive to ponder the evidence.

In Baldridge's analysis of 703 attacks, the victims' apparel is broken down as follows:

Partial	566
Wetsuits	60
Nude	53
Fully clothed	24

It is certainly no surprise that most victims were in bathing suits or otherwise partially clothed. However, it *is* surprising that 8 percent were nude because one would imagine that many fewer than 8 out of 100 bathers swim nude. However, a variety of cultures are represented in these worldwide statistics, including many where nude bathing is quite common. Then, too, in the English-speaking countries where most of the official records have originated, nude bathing might be done under what we have learned are dangerous circumstances: with little company, in deeper water, and at night. Also, white sunbathers who remove their suits to swim *au naturel* would expose areas of high contrast.

Since most people wear something when swimming, it behooves us to explain the effects of various colors of apparel. There are infinite variations in color and style of bathing suits, and the preferences of people change continually. Since there is little data control for this subject (what the masses of nonvictims wear has not been studied), it is difficult if not impossible to derive any conclusions from the colors and patterns of bathing suits and other gear and equipment either carried or worn by shark attack victims. This difficulty, of course, has not prevented speculation.

One expert found that, of 151 attacks (mostly from 1941 to 1968) where color combinations were reported, 72 percent of the victims displayed dark background colors (blue, brown, green, red, etc.) with lighter contrasting shades (white, yellow, tan, etc.) as opposed to light background colors with darker contrasting shades or patterns. It could easily be argued, however, that this trend reflects the color preference of the bathers rather than that of the sharks.

Information on the pattern of clothing worn during shark attack was available in 196 cases in the official records. Of these, 154 victims (79 percent) were believed to have been wearing plain clothing. Patterned clothing (including stripes) was noted in only 42 cases (21 percent). Therefore, the often repeated contention that patterned clothing is shark bait should be dismissed until significant evidence is offered.

The strongest argument that the colors or patterns of bathing suits are not important factors in attracting a shark or exciting it to attack is based on the very low incidence of damage to the region of the body normally covered by a bathing costume (only about 13 percent of tabulated injuries).

Though we cannot find meaningful correlations between the incidence of shark attack and the colors of bathing suits reportedly worn by victims, tests involving survival gear of different colors have clearly demonstrated that sharks have a predilection for attacking objects with a bright, contrasting, and/or reflective

appearance, including bright orange-yellows. Shark researchers have coined the term "yum-yum yellow" for International Orange and all the other bright yellow and orange-yellow colors used for sea-survival equipment such as life jackets and rafts. Yum-yum yellow is used because it contrasts strongly with the color of the sea, and thus enables searching aircraft and vessels to sight a man adrift at sea. But unfortunately, yum-yum yellow seems to be as conspicuous to sharks as to man. In tests, a standard yellow life vest on a child dummy was repeatedly attacked at the surface by Blue Sharks, while strikes on a nearby red one were very few and a black one suffered only two. Mako Sharks tore an arm from the yellow-jacketed dummy and one of them swallowed it. But the Makos made no attacks on either red or black vests.

Diver James Hay's yellow wetsuit was a likely factor in the five-second shark attack he suffered on December 4, 1959, while diving for abalone in murky waters three-quarters of a mile off Bodega Head, California. Hay, who was unharmed, later described the attack as follows: "I felt a tremendous shake and then a wiggling motion . . . it shook me back and forth under the water . . . then the creature let go." He returned safely to the island; a gashed swim fin and twisted ankle served as grim reminders of his narrow escape. (C #554)

In tests at sea with wild sharks, researchers experimenting with a shark screen found that the reflectivity of its surface was important. The shark screen is a large bag, open at the top, that floats on the surface of the sea. A castaway is safe in shark-infested waters in such a bag because it does not allow the smell of blood or body chemicals to escape into the sea, and it contains and protects the person's limbs. When the researchers made these bags of white or, particularly, of shiny material, the incidence of approaches and contacts increased. The conclusion is that shiny objects attract sharks.

Behavior of Persons Attacked

Bathers who become victims of beach-prowling sharks may appear, at first check, to have been engaging in no special or different activities—they were wading, swimming, floating, or playing water games just like the rest of the people at the beach. Yet when one studies the statistics and explores the subtle relationships between case histories, one discovers that sharks are more prone to attack people who are swimming than people who are engaged in other water sports. There is, according to H. David Baldridge, "the strong suggestion that movements by a swimmer may very well play a role in his being selected for attack by a shark." Moreover, it seems certain that some modes of swimming are particularly attractive to the predators. A case in point is that of sixteen-year-old Joseph Troy who was struck and killed while swimming only 10 feet away from an older companion in Buzzards Bay, Massachusetts, on July 26, 1936. Troy was using a vigorous crawl stroke, while his partner was sidestroking smoothly through the water. The suggestion is that the extra water disturbance caused by the crawl led the shark to attack. (C #222)

Robert Clark of Cocoa Beach, Florida, is typical of one class of victims selected for attack from beach populations. On the Fourth of July, 1975, Clark was paddling his surfboard about 50 feet off the beach when "I felt a sharp pain, so I pulled my leg away and started paddling as quickly as I could to shore. I never did see the shark." However, other swimmers spotted it and estimated it to be about 6 feet long. Clark underwent surgery to repair the deep wound and the damaged tendons on his foot. Doctors said he would be in a cast for a month. The beaches remained open.

The salient point of the attack on Clark is that he was paddling a surfboard at the time—hands and feet splashing in the water, the rest of his body screened from the shark. The attack was likely an instinctual response of the shark, stimulated by the swimming motions, not the work of a hungry animal looking for a meal. This theory is reinforced by the discovery on the next day, July 5, 1975, of the drowned body of William Fowler of Melbourne, Florida, who had disappeared at the same time and place where Clark was struck. Fowler's body, which one presumes was submerged in those same waters overnight, showed no wounds or other signs of attack. The shark would have had no problem finding Fowler and ravaging his body if it was hungry for human flesh.

In reviewing many other accounts from the official records, one finds case after case in which surfboards, air mattresses, beach rafts, and other flotation devices were being used by the victim. My contention is that people on these floating devices kick and paddle in a manner that is peculiarly attractive to sharks. Perhaps the sonic detectors of the attackers interpret the splashes as sounds of disabled fish or other vulnerable prey. Recent studies have shown that recorded sounds of struggling fish do serve as effective shark attractants and excitants. It is also quite possible that sharks perceive a large dark shape with hands and feet protruding from it as a swimming sea turtle.

In a typical case where a floating device was involved, fifteen-year-old Billy Weaver was attacked three-quarters of a mile from the shore at Oahu, Hawaii. He and five friends had been swimming and surfing near a reef on December 13, 1958, when Weaver, on a floating air mattress, failed to catch the wave the others caught and remained alone. Suddenly screams for help split the air and his companions wheeled around to see Weaver thrashing about, still clinging to the mattress. By the time they swam the 50 yards to where he struggled, his leg was gone and the water was cloudy with blood. Suddenly a shark surfaced 30 feet away from them. Frightened, they launched Weaver's floating body toward a reef nearby, and swam rapidly for their anchored boat. But the body was gone by the time the boys got the boat back to the scene. Finally on the next day, an organized search found his body lodged below in the reef. The attacker, estimated to be 15 feet or longer, remained at the scene, patrolling the waters above the reef during recovery. In the next few days, two Tiger Sharks, 11 and 12 feet long, were captured in the area during an intensive hunt for the killer. (C #405)

Persons entering the water abruptly by leaping or falling are often struck immediately, almost as if the shark were lying in wait. The sudden violent entry into the water of a human body may be perceived by a nearby shark as a threat to which it instinctively responds with viciously aggressive behavior. Or, the reaction may be an opportunistic hunger response to the sudden presence of a potential meal.

The official records show that sharks respond negatively when aggressive action is taken against them. While most shark attacks (86 percent) are not associated with any known provocative acts on the part of the victims, those who did become victims of "subsequent acts of elicited resentment on the part of the sharks," as Baldridge calls them, had seized, kicked, struck, hooked, netted, or speared their attackers. Persons have been struck by sharks while rescuing a victim, and keepers have been bitten while doing research with or feeding captive sharks.

Attacking a large shark under almost any circumstances will lead to trouble. Spearfisherman Tony Dicks almost became the victim of his own curiosity and foolish aggression in an encounter with a 9-foot Great White Shark on May 30, 1959, near Port Elizabeth, South Africa. Dicks and a companion saw the shark swimming in the area and approached it for a closer look. The shark, returning their curiosity, swam toward them. Dicks then fired a spear from his gas-powered gun into the shark's body, and suddenly found himself being towed rapidly away by the wounded creature on the other end of his spear cable. Suddenly the shark wheeled to attack him, jaws open, teeth flashing. Dicks jammed his unloaded spear gun down the shark's throat and, firing a blast of gas, leaped onto the monster's back. His companion then entered the fight and killed the attacker with one deadly shot right through its gills. (C #382)

The data strongly suggest that sharks are prone to attack isolated swimmers, as in the case of Billy Weaver. In 34 percent of analyzed attack cases, there was no one near the victim. In 40 percent of them, there was one companion or more within 50 feet of the victim.

The vulnerability of the lone swimmer is typified in an Australian case involving nineteen-year-old Maxwell Steele. One afternoon he and some companions were waiting to catch a wave about 100 yards from shore at North Bondi near Sydney. Steele missed a wave that the others had caught. He was struck in the leg, pulled under the surface by a shark, and dragged a good distance through the water. He survived.

Another case of a swimmer attacked after being left alone occurred in Panama near a small island. Three boys saw what they thought was a log lying on the bottom. Two of the boys quit after three dives, thinking that the log might be a shark. The third boy stayed to make a last dive and was struck once by a 6-foot shark while still submerged. It then attacked him again before the other boys could pull him into a nearby boat. The result was fatal.

An important, and as yet unresolved, matter is the reason why a shark picks one particular victim from among a variety of potential targets. To date, the question "Why that particular person out of hundreds at the beach?" remains unanswered by science, at least in cases where the victim was not engaged in some especially attractive behavior.

Spearfishers are the victims of about 20 percent of all recorded attacks. This should be no surprise because spear fishing often brings man and shark into close contact under conditions where the shark is excited by the presence of wounded fish. Aggression against a man under such conditions might be an attempt on the part of the shark to drive away a potential competitor for available food rather than any attempt to actually feed upon the man.

Attack Against Divers

The evidence that scuba and skin divers are particularly vulnerable to attack is very convincing, even though much of it is circumstantial. This finding contradicts the widely held belief that totally submerged persons are less susceptible to shark attack than swimmers at the surface.

As would be expected in view of the relatively recent rise in popularity of all forms of sport diving, most reported attacks involving divers have occurred since 1950, and they appear to be increasing. At present, there are 244 official records of shark attacks on divers; they comprise one-fifth of the entire case file.

Only one of the 244 attacks was against a female diver. This was the case of Fiji Island spearfisher Asena, who was attacked at the surface after diving for fish. Furthermore, no report of attack on any female beneath the surface of the water has ever been reported in the official case files.

Is this because female skin divers behave differently in the water than male skin divers, swimming with a movement that is less exciting to sharks, or is it because they give off a different odor that does not invite shark attack? Perhaps, but a more likely explanation is that few female skin divers spearfish, pry abalone from rocks in waters inhabited by large sharks, or tie bleeding fish to their belts—all activities that have been reported in association with shark attacks on male skin divers.

The high danger to divers is probably related to their habit of going greater distances from shore than most swimmers. In 115 analyzed cases, 76 percent of diver victims were more than 200 feet from shore. As for depth, the distribution of attacks is probably determined more by the divers' preferences than by sharks'.

Because of the suddenness of attack, the opacity of the water, and the panic that normally ensues, it is often difficult to get from witnesses a reliable identification of the species of the attacker. However, teeth marks in the victim and the apparent jaw configuration are sometimes conclusive enough to permit identification. In ninety-four recorded cases of attack on divers, the sharks have been recognized. The most notorious attackers are the Tiger Shark (twelve attacks), the White Shark (eleven), the Mako (seven), and the Hammerhead (three).

One strong cause-and-effect relation stands out clearly among the correlations between shark attack and diver activity—*underwater spearfishing attracts sharks*. More than one out of every four shark attacks recorded since 1958 has been on a spearfisher. This activity—by both scuba divers and skin divers using mask, snorkel, and fins—accounted for four-fifths of the diver victims in the official records. Of 103 skin divers attacked, 80 percent were engaged in spearfishing and 51 percent had captive fish in their possession when struck.

There is no doubt that sharks are strongly attracted to fish blood and whatever other fluids or chemicals that might be given off by wounded or frightened fish. That is only natural, for scenting vulnerable prey is part of the normal feeding habits of sharks. Sharks will strike essentially anything that has

been treated with fish "juice." In one experiment, Lemon Sharks were induced to repeatedly strike a cellulose sponge that was dipped in fish body fluids. Dead rats were eaten only when their fur was wetted with fish blood.

These experiments and the direct evidence in the records provide a convincing argument that spearfishers who keep captured fish close at hand on a stringer, in a nearby float, or tied to their belts are foolishly exposing themselves to attack. In attacks on persons who had attached captured fish to their belts, the shark often appeared to be directing its strike at the tethered fish rather than the man—though the result was often fatal to the man.

A typical case is that of Len Jones, who had a narrow escape from the jaws of a 10-foot White Shark. He was spearfishing along the South Africa coast and had just surfaced with two 8-pound fish on his belt and was about to spear a third when he was suddenly pitched violently upward. Looking down, he saw "the pectorals (of the shark) sticking out at the sides and shaking." Punching and pushing at the attacking shark, Jones fought free, relatively uninjured. His two fish and the diving knife attached to his belt were missing—the shark's only reward. (C #1452)

Almost 17 percent of victims in the official records since 1958 were wearing some form of wetsuit. Westsuits, of course, are primarily worn by skin divers, and skin divers expose themselves to shark attack to a much higher degree than do individuals who populate the beaches and seashores in general. But the high percentage might be explained, at least in part, by the wetsuit itself. It is not unreasonable to suppose that a person clad in a wetsuit resembles a seal or other marine animal upon which sharks might feed, especially if the water is murky and the range of vision limited. This sort of mistaken identity would explain why in a number of attacks by White Sharks on men in wetsuits, the sharks have quickly released and deserted their victims after initial sudden assaults.

The case of twenty-three-year-old abalone hunter Robert Rebstock is an example. On July 23, 1975, Rebstock and three companions were warned by commercial fishermen that they had seen a huge 16-foot Great White Shark in the area a mile north of Point Conception near Santa Barbara, California. Suspecting the fishermen were trying to coax them away from the abalone beds, the young men moved only a mile north along the coast, where the seals they sighted reassured them that the waters were indeed free of sharks. They then anchored their boat.

Rebstock was the first to don his gear and plunge beneath the surface. Dressed in a black wetsuit with rubber swim fins, face mask, and scuba tank, he swam down for a quick reconnaissance of the rocky bottom and then ascended to get his abalone iron from the boat. Just as he broke the surface the White Shark struck.

"My feet went right down his throat," Rebstock said later. His roommate, who witnessed the attack from the boat, stated, "It came up in a rush with Rob in its mouth, straight up out of the water—maybe three feet or so—then it just dropped him and we grabbed him out of the water and took off." Rebstock was rushed to a nearby hospital where he was treated for lacerations, a gash on his right thigh, and puncture wounds on his left leg. "I'm lucky to be alive," he said. Rebstock was right. Once in the maw of a 16-foot shark, one is indeed lucky to escape. Analyzing the case, one sees an error in the divers' logic. Seals in the area would attract sharks. It is probable that, seeing a large black creature swimming in a manner so unlike a fish, the shark rushed to the attack, expecting a mouthful of seal. When the bite proved to taste of unpalatable rubber, the shark spit the diver out and swam off looking for the real thing.

Divers have better range of vision than bathers. In 108 cases where the attacker was seen before the strike, 60 percent involved divers and only 30 percent bathers. Divers also made more numerous observations of the normal and circling movements of sharks than bathers. By the very nature of their activity, divers are more observant than bathers, and hence their reports of a good deal of preattack circling by sharks are probably more accurate than the testimony of bathers who noted no circling before an attack.

Diver victims were set upon suddenly and violently in 73 percent of 113 analyzed cases. Most often the sharks made controlled and deliberate single strikes. In one of every eight cases, the shark released its initial hold and very quickly bit the victim again as though to get a better grip. The behavior of sharks making multiple strikes on divers was classed as "frenzied" about one-fourth of the time.

The marauder that suddenly and violently attacked fifty-three-year-old Donald Joslin was a Great White Shark at least 14 feet long. The place was 300 yards northwest of Tomales Point, California, in an area where fishermen had seen a large shark the previous day. It was September 6, 1969, and Joslin was 25 feet down in clear water fishing abalone when he was hit with sudden violence: "There was a viselike pressure on my lower leg raising me up and completely out of the water. 'Shark!' I yelled and fell back with a twisting motion onto the shark's back." The force of his fall ripped the diver's leg free from the shark's jaws, tearing a 4-inch gash, breaking the bone, and cutting numerous tendons and nerves. Joslin continued: "I hurriedly refitted my face mask, cleared it, and looked down just in time to see the persistent shark turning to strike again." He met this charge by straight-arming the beast with his abalone iron. Again, the impact of the charge threw him half out of the water. Mustering past experience (in the rescue of diver Robert French in 1962), Joslin prepared for the next round. In his gloved hand he had his abalone iron ready, and "when its head broke water, I cut loose with an overhead right putting all the strength I could muster into it." The injured shark spun away while Joslin was quickly hauled aboard a rescue boat for treatment. (C #1647)

Because they are better able to observe and escape sharks than bathers, divers have suffered repeat attacks in only one of twelve cases, whereas bathers have suffered repeat attacks in about one out of five cases.

Because it is a general safety rule with divers to use the "buddy system," potential rescuers are close at hand in a high percentage of incidents. Thus in the accounts of attacks on divers, we see numerous examples of rescuers going immediately to the aid of the victim. The rescuers have actually fought the shark, and on occasion even placed themselves as barriers between the attacker and its victim.

Injury to the lower parts of the body occurred far less often to divers than to swimmers and waders. This is understandable because swimmers usually splash with their feet, water treaders dangle their moving legs from the surface, and waders usually submerge only the lower half of their bodies. Injury to the upper parts of the body are about as frequent for divers as for bathers.

The injuries to divers are typically less severe than those to bathers. Many fewer arms and legs are lost, there is a lower rate of lost tissue, and a much lower death rate than for swimmers and waders. The reasons are obvious: divers have a better opportunity to see an attack coming, and their spear guns give them a much greater ability to fight one off once it is in progress. The preponderant majority who use the buddy system also have effective assistance at hand.

Extraordinary coolness under attack is a hallmark of practiced divers. They are prepared by experience and fortified by a habit of self-reliance to protect their lives and defeat their attackers. Again and again, submerged divers emerge alive after grueling contests with White Sharks, Tiger Sharks, and other notorious maneaters. They have improved on the normal one-to-one odds of survival for swimmers to the degree that they have earned a twelve-to-one chance of survival.

How divers raise their survival odds is shown by Brian Rodger, a veteran spearfisher in a team contest at Aldinga Reef, about 30 miles from Adelaide, South Australia, on March 12, 1961. Rodger had been chasing fish for about three hours and was out of sight of the other divers. He was swimming about three-quarters of a mile offshore in a depth of 30 feet of water, towing 50 pounds of fish behind him on a float, when suddenly he was seized by his left leg. Twisting quickly around, he saw a 12-foot White Shark clamped to his leg. Rodger swung hard, hoping to ram the shark's eye. Just then it released his leg. His fist and arm went right between the jaws and straight down the huge throat. Startled, the shark released its grasp, withdrew, and circled to attack again. Rodger dived and fired a spear directly into the shark's head, which penetrated 2 or 3 inches. The shark, now on the defensive, turned and swam away, leaving the diver bleeding profusely from arm and leg lacerations. (C #842)

Badly wounded and bleeding severely, Rodger managed to fashion a tourniquet for his left thigh by twisting his diving knife through the power cords of his spear gun. Still towing his catch, he slowly began to swim for shore, weakening rapidly. Reluctantly ditching his weights and spear gun and releasing his fish, he half-floated and half-swam on his back, heading for a distant reef. His frequent yells and waves for help finally caught the attention of some fellow divers in a boat. He survived and curiously, his abandoned catch was recovered by his teammates. The extra 50 pounds was the deciding factor in their winning the contest.

Attack Against Boats

It is hard to imagine anything more frightening to a boater than a spontaneous violent attack by a huge shark. Few boaters are prepared to handle an assault that combines the instant threat of drowning with the dark terror of mutilation by a shark. Boats have been ripped open, disabled, capsized, and lifted from the water in various incidents. While such attacks are certainly fearful when they happen, not more than five or ten are recorded in the course of each year.

The official attack records list 168 boat incidents around the world. Many of them were provoked by people in the boats, who, for example, had hooked or harpooned a shark and had then lost control of it. But many more occurred spontaneously and without apparent provocation. Whether provoked or unprovoked, the shark usually appears to be motivated by pure aggression and the desire to destroy the boat rather than to destroy its human occupants. This seems to be true even for the few instances where the force of the attack carried the shark over the gunwales and into the boat.

The aggression theory is supported by many cases where the boat sank or the occupants were thrown into the water but were not molested by the attacking shark. A dramatic example of this was recorded off Nova Scotia in 1953 as the finale of a prolonged episode involving two fishermen in a 12-foot dory and a White Shark of equal length. For several days, off and on, the shark had followed the dory, the only one with a white-painted bottom then operating out of the port of Forchu, Cape Breton Island. Finally, the shark attacked the bottom of the dory with violence and ripped away enough planking to swamp it and to cast both fishermen into the sea. Despite its persistent tracking and violent aggression against the dory, the shark attacked neither of the fishermen, although both were in the water for several hours and one eventually drowned.

On other occasions, sharks are more casual in their aggression against boats. Consider this incident off Cape Lookout, North Carolina, in 1905, as related by observer Russell J. Coles in Norman and Fraser's *Giant Fishes, Whales and Dolphins:*

" It apparently had no fear of us as it struck the side of the skiff with some force. It then swam away for a distance of several hundred yards, then turned and swam rapidly towards us. I was about to fire into it as a large loggerhead turtle arose to the surface and was attacked by the shark. The shark seized the turtle in its jaws and both disappeared beneath the surface. The next day I harpooned this turtle and found the upper shell for a width of nearly 30 inches showing the marks of the shark's teeth. The edge of the shell and the right hind flipper had been torn away. "

Sharks attack almost every type of craft up to 40 feet or longer—launches, dinghies, power boats, sailboats, canoes, and rafts—but most assaults are on craft smaller than 20 feet. Sharks bite oars, propellers, rudders, rails, planks, and keels. They occasionally leap inside boats. The identity of the attacker is often learned by expert examination of teeth removed from the hull of the boat, and its size is deduced from the spacing of the tooth marks. Shark experts can also re-create details of the pattern of attack and the angle of strike from the position of the jaw imprint on the boat.

A three-quarters of an inch long tooth fragment embedded in the woodwork of a fishing boat was the calling card left by a large White Shark (called a Blue Pointer locally) in False Bay, Cape Province, South Africa. Fishing had been good on an October day in 1960 when a shark was sighted circling the boat. The concerned captain ordered the fishing stopped, but an unaware crewman continued to fish and hooked a bluefish (shad locally). The shark was lured by the fish, rushed at it, missed, smashed into the gunwale of the boat, and fell back into the sea. Then, just as the boat

was about to move off, the frustrated shark suddenly attacked at great speed, biting viciously into the side of the craft. The 18-inch hole it ripped was above the watermark, fortunately, and the boat sailed safely into port.

Sharks that attack boats are usually loners but gang attacks do occur occasionally. Among the records, I have found two incidents involving three and six sharks, respectively, in the waters off eastern Australia.

Australia certainly holds the record for shark attacks on boats; 50 percent of all the incidents officially recorded have occurred along its eastern coast. The United States is next, with 25 percent of recorded attacks. (This follows the general geography of attack statistics, in that Australia and the United States also have the highest number of attacks on persons.) South Africa and New Zealand followed in the statistics with about 6 and 3 percent, respectively. And consideration of a particular section of coastline often indicates that sharks are more prone to attack boats in places not frequented by bathers or divers.

Many scientific experts have studied boat attacks. French shark expert Paul Budker, pondering the mystery of boat attacks in his book, *The Life of Sharks,* makes the following observations:

" The Mako . . . seems to be particularly addicted to this type of aggressiveness, although it is known too in the Tiger Shark and the Whale Shark, if not to the same extent. What can it be that impels a shark to attack an object so inedible as the hull of a boat? It is unlikely that its sensory equipment, olfactory or otherwise, persuades it that it has chanced on a good prey to eat, for this type of encounter often ends badly for the shark. It may leave some teeth implanted in the wood or else knock itself senseless on impact, for sharks have been observed to swim headlong and at full speed straight into a boat, damaging ribs and planking.

One may well question whether it is hunger that drives sharks to attack boats. The comparison might be made with a mongrel dog chasing a bicycle, barking at it like mad; it is unlikely that the mongrel intends eating the cyclist. There is no doubt that hunger is not the only possible explanation, although it certainly must rank top of the list from time to time. . . . Possibly, sharks in a state of sexual activity are more irritable, more aggressive. The problem does not seem to have been tackled from this point of view, although experimental studies would be extremely difficult to carry out. **" "**

Identification of Attacker

One means of positively identifying an attacker is recognition of the human remains in its stomach. Such proof has been reported in nineteen out of thirty-four official cases where absolute identification was made. One of these concerned Navy Commander John Gibson, on a day's outing with Donna Waugh in Magens Bay, St. Thomas, Virgin Islands, on April 20, 1963. While Gibson started a long swim across the Bay, Donna walked slowly along the shore. As she reached the shore on the far side, she saw Gibson thrashing in the water with one hand already missing. Over his protestations, she quickly swam to his aid, and as she was dragging him toward shore, the shark continued to mangle Gibson's body. Rescuers got the remains into a skiff but Gibson was dead or dying from the severance of the femoral artery in his right thigh. The next afternoon, intensive fishing produced a 10-foot Galapagos Shark (the first one of the species ever seen in the Atlantic) with Gibson's missing hand and other body parts in its stomach.

Because human flesh remains undigested and in a good state of preservation for a time in the shark's stomach, identification can often be accomplished several days after an attack. This observation indicates that we know very little about the digestive system of a shark. For example, it was five days after Mary Passaris lost her arm in an attack that the limb, with her finger ring still in place, was recovered in good condition from the stomach of a 9-foot Australian Whaler Shark. Passaris had been struck 30 feet offshore, near Broome in western Australia, on May 16, 1949.

Another sure method of identifying the attacker species works when the culprit has left a tooth in the victim. The tooth, or even a fragment of it, can be reliably used for identification because each species has teeth of a unique shape and structure. Even such close relatives as the White Shark, Mako Shark, and the Porbeagle can be distinguished by comparing details of tooth structure. Wounds of the victims are often X-rayed in the hope of locating a fragment of tooth large enough to permit identification of the species of shark responsible for the injury. In nineteen of the official attack cases, tooth fragments were recovered, and in twelve, there was positive identification.

X-ray photographs of Petrus Sithole's extensive wounds revealed shark tooth fragments that established the identity of the young man's killer. On December 25, 1960, Sithole, a twenty-five-year-old African house servant, had been swimming 200 feet from shore in brown murky water outside the shark enclosure at Margate, South Africa, that was reserved for "Europeans." At 4:30 P.M., the attacker struck. Sithole screamed, flailed the water with his arms, and half-rose out of the sea. Ignored by the beach folks and bypassed by two fleeing fellow swimmers, Sithole slipped beneath the blood-reddened waters. Not until the victim washed close to shore did a man run to the water and drag the torso onto the beach. Both legs had been cleanly amputated by the attacker. The tooth fragments that were located by X-ray proved to be those of a 9-foot Bull Shark (called Zambezi locally) weighing about 400 pounds.

In typical detective style, experts have also been successful in identifying the attacker species by comparing the appearance of the wounds to the anatomy and dentition of particular sharks. For example, the saw-toothed triangular teeth of the White Shark cut neat gouges in a victim's flesh that appear quite different from the shreds left by the Mako Shark.

My colleague, Eugenie Clark, when with the Mote Marine Laboratory in Sarasota used a variety of preserved jaws to make bites in soft clay and then matched the impressions against the appearance of the victim's wounds. Dr. Clark used this technique to determine that the attacker of Douglas Lawton was a Tiger Shark and not a Bull Shark. On July 27, 1966, Douglas and his brother were swimming in 4 feet of water off a Sarasota beach when a shark seized his leg and pulled him down. While the brother kept his head above water and both boys tried to beat off the shark, his parents and an aunt and uncle rushed to help. With the uncle and father tugging on it, the shark finally let go and swam away. The shark, which had attacked less than 10 feet from shore, had mauled the boy's leg so badly that only amputation could save him.

Tiger Sharks were identified as the attackers in 27 of 257 verified cases, exceeding all other species but one in worldwide attack frequency. As one would expect, the White Shark holds the record with thirty-two verified attacks to date (case files are complete to the end of 1968). The species-verified attacks by the world's most dangerous sharks are as follows:

Great White Shark	32
Tiger Shark	27
Bull Shark	22
Whaler Shark	20
Grey Nurse Shark	19
Mako Shark	18
Hammerhead Shark	13
Sand Tiger (Ragged-Tooth) Shark	11
Blacktip Shark	8
Lemon Shark	6

(BALDRIDGE, CONTRIBUTIONS FROM THE MOTE MARINE LABORATORY)

Reaction

In the wake of any act of violence, the human reaction is to find the villain and wreak vengeance, or at least demand an explanation. So the attacker shark must be caught, killed, examined for evidence, and the corpse displayed in order to satisfy the public demand for revenge. That is why a shark hunt will be mobilized as soon as the initial shock of attack passes if there are boats and competent fishermen about. The official records list 114 such hunts, which resulted in the capture and execution of 64 culprits. The captured shark was positively identified as the villain in about half of successful hunts.

The death of Billy Weaver in Hawaii was followed by an extensive campaign of extermination, as was the New Jersey rogue shark incident of 1916. In the latter case, the third and final round of terrifying

attacks—two people killed and a third injured—was countered by one of the most intensive shark hunts ever undertaken. An army of shark hunters launched an offensive, using spears, nets, and baited hooks. They fired thousands of rounds of ammunition into any place they thought the shark could be hiding. Hour after hour, sharks were dragged ashore and killed. Finally, after two days of exhaustive war, an 8½-foot shark caught off South Amboy, New Jersey, yielded from its stomach a mass of human flesh and bones. The villain was identified by naturalist John Treadwell Nichols as a White Shark.

But sometimes sharks are not treated with vengeance, even by their victims. A small Nurse Shark bit spearfisher Donald Ritter near Key West, Florida, on August 7, 1967, and refused to relinquish his thigh, even after being dragged ashore by the victim with the help of companion Robert Hughes. There it was dislodged by the two men. Indulging in a bit of scientific investigation, they then weighed it (28 pounds), measured it (3½ feet), checked its sex (male), put an identification tag on it, and let it go.

This event notwithstanding, shark attack is normally a raw test of the most basic human strengths and weaknesses. All the trappings of civilization and all the rationality we pride ourselves on dissolve in the first seconds of violence. There is no time to consider, only time to react. The test is primal man against primal beast.

The bravest type of human reaction is illustrated in the case of Albert Kogler who was attacked on May 7, 1959, at Baker Beach, California, at about 5:30 P.M. Kogler, eighteen, and his companion, Shirley O'Neill, had been swimming about 50 yards from the shore in calm, clear water. Just as they were about to return to the beach, Kogler suddenly screamed and began to struggle, warning O'Neill, "It's a shark—get out of here!" She retreated a few strokes, then turned to see blood everywhere. "He just kept screaming and screaming. I could tell that the fish was chewing him up. He was shouting: 'Help me, Help me!' " Rushing to his rescue, she grabbed for his hand and found that "his arm was just hanging there by a thread." She finally got hold of his body and began to struggle shoreward as people gathered on the beach to watch the action. When they were 10 feet from shore, a fisherman finally threw a line out to them. Efforts to save Kogler at a nearby hospital failed. At no time during her daring rescue attempt did the shark try to attack O'Neill.

In 270 attempted rescue cases in the official files, only 3 rescuers died; 9 were injured but escaped death. Thus, as a rescuer, you have a 99 percent chance to escape alive and a 97 percent chance to escape injury. These odds, of course, are of more comfort to a reader than to a potential rescuer faced with the choice between fear and duty.

Consider, for example, the case of Sailasa Ratubalavu, who was holding a speared fish near a reef 5 miles from Fiji on May 8, 1964. Ignoring six companions, a Tiger Shark struck Ratubalavu without warning, shearing off the man's buttocks. As Ratubalavu screamed in agony, the shark tore away at his lower abdomen. Five panicked divers raced toward their boat, moored some distance away. One remained to help drive off the shark and to drag the victim to safety. After swimming for nearly forty-five minutes with Ratubalavu on his back, the lone rescuer managed to reach the boat and the other divers. Brought aboard, Ratubalavu asked the others to care for his wife and children and then died. (C #1299)

One would assume that experienced divers are more effective rescuers than sunbathers or casual swimmers. The assumption is confirmed by many incidents, such as that of Roy Pinder and a fellow spearfisher, who were attacked by a persistent 6-foot Springer Shark near Spanish Wells in the Bahamas in June 1968. The shark had been harassing the divers by making fast rushes into the water where they had speared fish; presumably the blood and gurry in the water had excited it. They moved a distance away and continued spearing fish. Pinder was surfacing with a speared grouper when the shark charged, first ramming him on the head and then clamping its jaws onto his skull. Freed by his companion, who jabbed the shark repeatedly with a spear, Pinder struggled back to the boat with the shark still after him. The maddened fish then turned on the rescuer, rushing him with open jaws. The man responded by firing a 5-foot spear directly into the shark's throat. As the shark thrashed about trying to dislodge the spear, the rescuer escaped to the safety of the boat.

Victims under ravaging attack usually scream repeatedly as the beast shakes and mutilates them. But victims of a single strike often feel little sensation of pain and are, in fact, unaware that they have been bitten. Little research has been done on this phenomenon. One interesting clue, however, was provided by the physician who conducted the autopsy on the corpse of Stanley Fisher, one of the New Jersey rogue shark's victims. The doctor was quoted as concluding that "the flesh torn by the maneater's teeth was impregnated with a peculiar poisonous liquid, which seemed to have a deadening effect on the nerves and muscles," and that "this probably explained why Fisher apparently had little sensation of pain when the shark took off his leg." (C #205)

The absence of immediate pain is exemplified by the case of Leroy French, who on November 11, 1962, was part of a group of thirty men and women skin divers anchored over a sunken reef off the Farallon Islands near San Francisco. French, age twenty-four, completed his dive and was swimming back to the boat when he

" felt a tug on my left arm. My first thought was that it was another diver letting me know he was there. I turned to see who it was and noticed a lot of blood in the water. I then saw an enormous tail swirling in the water and knew it was a shark. It let go of my arm and then I felt it grab my leg, but before it pulled me under I managed to get a couple of yells out for help. As I was pulled under (about 15 feet), I started stabbing the shark in the area of its head with my spear gun—it was squirming and biting all the way down my leg to the ankle. " (C #1115)

The relevant point is that *French did not realize that he had been bitten until after he saw the shark.* Apparently, the shark bit French first on the left arm and hand, then on the right buttock and left calf, and finally on the right knee. At this point, the attacking 14-foot White Shark fled and French was pulled into a boat from which he was picked up by a Coast Guard helicopter and flown to a hospital. It was this efficient rescue operation that saved his life and enabled him to tell his own story.

Motive for Attack

Our most disturbing fears about sharks are rooted in the inexplicable. Where the reason for attack is not evident, fear rushes in to fill the vacuum. Although shark experts are often unable to provide a specific reason for a particular attack, they have reached certain conclusions that are helpful.

First, it can be stated emphatically that sharks do not routinely go about attacking people in order to fill their stomachs. In fact, the evidence shows that aggression, defense, and mistaken identity are the more likely motives in most attacks. Because sharks are biologically geared to feed on fish, seals, turtles, and other aquatic life, they do not prey on humans except under unusual circumstances. Swimmers and divers regularly frequent the same waters as sharks, and often within sight of them, without incident.

Nevertheless, the motivating factor behind a shark attack on man was once assumed to be hunger, for in many cases of predation, the human victim was either partially or totally eaten by the shark. The occasional findings of human remains in the stomachs of sharks were readily accepted as confirmation of this theory. Yet there is mounting evidence to show that the drive may not be as important as it was once believed to be.

While sharks are effective predators and could take hunks of flesh without effort if that were their wish, the amount of flesh taken from a human victim is small in most cases. Photographs and descriptions of lacerations show that most wounds are from tooth raking and slashing rather than from chopping. Consequently, we see severe cuts and slashes in most victims but not a significant loss of tissue.

The official records show that the majority of shark attacks on humans are single encounters wherein the shark strikes once, leaving a single wound or set of wounds. The attack is often preceded by one or two practice runs, but the shark normally stops after the first actual strike, making no attempt to follow up and devour its victim. If hunger motivates the initial strike, either the taste or the feel of human flesh discourages the shark from further adventure.

The first strike can be fatal, though, as shown by the case of native spearfisher Titus Tiso of Samarai, Papua, who was approached by a Tiger Shark while clutching a fish in his hand. Tiso was heard to shout in terror at sight of the shark so deliberately and slowly swimming toward him, its huge fin cutting the water. It ignored the fish and attacked Tiso, ripping off his left arm, shoulder, and heart with a single bite. Death was instantaneous. The body was not further attacked and was recovered shortly thereafter in 10 feet of water. The same shark appears to have attacked and killed a second victim in the same area on the following day.

Fish thrown overside, or fish blood and gurry flowing into the sea, attracts sharks and often excites them to a frenzy of feeding. It certainly seems senseless to enter the water in such circumstances, yet this is exactly what spearfishers do, often at great risk to their lives.

A favorite trouble spot for them is Point Aulone near Pacific Grove, California. Barry Wilson was killed by a White Shark here in 1952. On February 6, 1966, in this same place, a bleeding 2-foot fish he had just speared appears to have lured the 15- to 20-foot White Shark that startled spearfisher James Jacobs. Coming up from the rear while he was lying prone on the surface, the shark ripped away his flippers and slashed the lower parts of his wetsuit. Jacobs kicked and the shark left.

My good friend, and diver par excellence, Stanley Meltzoff found that sharks are the main drawback to spearfishing at the southern end of the barrier reef on British Honduras. Says Stan, "It is so usual for a speared fish to be taken from the diver that only those hunting shark will find fishing profitable."

Another colleague, shark expert Donald Nelson, confirms this difficulty in "Meeting the Shark Underwater" from *Underwater Naturalist:* "Sharks can locate speared fish from relatively long distances by both sound and smell. Spearfishermen of the tropical reef areas know that sharks often appear shortly after fish have been speared, especially if the fish are not boated immediately. It is not rare for a diver to have his fish, and sometimes his spear and gun along with it, taken by a shark."

In 941 cases of all types of fishing activity

analyzed by H. David Baldridge, where the presence of captured fish was noted, about one victim in five possessed fish with him at the time of attack. He argues that considering the very low proportion of people in the water who are carrying dead fish around, the fact that such persons make up almost a fifth of all known victims of shark attack points strongly to the foolishness of keeping a bleeding, struggling, or dead fish anywhere near one's person in waters where the presence of a shark is even a remote possibility.

Following another line of investigation, I was a bit disappointed to find that the statisticians who analyzed the Navy case files excluding castaways did not find human blood to be a powerful attractant to sharks. This idea has been prevalent for so many years, it would have been reassuring to have it confirmed. The facts show that of the more than 1,000 official cases studied, in only 31 (3 percent) is there a strong possibility that the blood of the victim or another human could have been the attractant. But it must be remembered that most people are in the water voluntarily when attacked, and only a miniscule number of them are bleeding heavily. Therefore, one would conclude that bleeders were six times more susceptible to attack.

So much for the routine attacks listed in the official shark files. The experience of dozens of survivors of sea disasters provides a strong case for the effect of human blood in attracting and inciting sharks. So obvious is the attraction and frenzied excitement of sharks in the presence of blood that castaways have always made every effort to prevent the seepage of blood or vomit from lifeboats and rafts and to vacate areas where these substances pervade the water.

Sharks are positively known to have the ability to detect minute amounts of blood in the water from many miles away. They are attracted in hope of finding some kind of food. Where there is blood there should be action. Maybe not always, but the chance is certainly worth the effort to the shark. And if the source turns out to be an unpalatable human, the shark will usually not linger looking for meat there. In short, sharks may be attracted often and yet attack rarely. It takes more than the presence of a human body to stimulate an attack and more than blood to prolong it. It takes a whole interacting combination of events, a combination that frightens people and frustrates scientists searching for reasonable explanations.

In considering another angle, the possible effect of human wastes, Baldridge states, "It can be realistically assumed, considering the numbers of people who populate the waters at resorts, that more than just a little human urine finds its way into the sea in the immediate vicinity of beaches." To test the possibility that urine could act as an attractant, researchers turned to their experimental sharks. In the tanks, Blacktip Sharks showed an awareness of the presence of human urine but were neither attracted nor repelled by it. Again, urine, like any chemical stimulus, may serve only to bring the shark to the scene, from which it would then normally depart in disappointment at not finding more appetizing prey. (In a tank, there would be no place to go.) Baldridge points to the possibility that awareness may be only the first link in a chain of response that terminates in attack.

Why sharks attack boats is by no means clear. The attacks on boats that are prompted by human provocation are motivated by self-defense and therefore involve little mystery. But unprovoked, aggressive attacks are another matter, particularly when they are directed against boats longer than 20 feet. In some attacks, the shark may have believed the boat to be a whale or some other large edible creature. Sharks do attack large prey and have little to fear in the way of counterattack from most of them.

Attacks on the boats of fishermen are less of a mystery because they so often are discharging odiferous substances that are known to attract sharks, such as the blood, slime, and body juices of the fish that have been caught or that are being used for bait. Even a small amount of such a substance discharged in a continuous trickle over a period of an hour or so may bring sharks close to the boat. Consequently, the sight of sharks gathering around a fishing boat at rest in the water is common enough. But an attack by these sharks against the boat is rare. Therefore, fishermen do not hesitate to pour masses of ground fish, blood, or other offal into the water currents to attract various fishes, and sometimes specifically to attract sharks to their hooks.

It is well known that sharks follow ships in order to feed on discarded foodstuff. They also abound along shorelines adjacent to dumping sites. For example, one night when I was operating the research vessel *Dolphin* out of the Sandy Hook Marine Laboratory, we caught 110 sharks on one set of our lines in the Hudson Canyon garbage dumping site off New York City. The suspected presence of such waste material was noted in nearly 25 percent of the analyzed attack cases. This clearly supports the contention that sharks are attracted by garbage and other wastes. Therefore, people should realize that to swim in waters where wastes are disposed heightens the risk of disaster. Certainly every effort should be made to stop the dumping of garbage and trash in coastal areas.

Animals, including pets, may be attractive to sharks, as Harry Goodridge of Rockport, Maine, discovered when an 11½-foot White Shark rose from the depths to swallow his pet seal Basil. The shark found Basil swimming around Goodridge's boat, bit him in two, and swallowed both halves. Goodridge angrily executed the shark with his harpoon and hauled it in from the sea, whereupon he found it had still another seal in its stomach.

The following account concerning an incident in Port Phillip, Australia, serves to further illustrate the point:

A specimen between 15 or 16 feet long had been observed for several days swimming around the ladies' baths, looking through the picket fence in such a disagreeable manner that the stationmaster had a strong hook and iron chain made so as to keep the rope out of reach of his teeth, and this, being baited with a large piece of pork made to look as much like a piece of lady as possible, was swallowed greedily, and then, with the aid of a crowd of helpers, the monster was got on shore. On opening the stomach, amongst a load of partially digested objects, a large Newfoundland dog was found, with his collar on, identifying him as one lost the day before, no doubt swallowed while enjoy-

ing a swim in the comparatively shallow water.

If there is a conclusion from all the preceding statistics, anecdotes, and interpretations, it is that shark motivation may be understandable in general but quite unpredictable in specific cases. And without a high degree of predictability for a foundation, researchers cannot provide a set of rules that will guarantee safety to all users of the sea. An uncertain and fearsome risk remains. Where motives such as hunger, self-defense, or momentary aggression may be ascribed, we feel comfortable and forewarned. But unaccountable acts of violence leave us shaken and anxious.

The most fearsome of deviants are those attackers designated "rogue sharks" by the experts. These are solitary sharks that are on the hunt for people. The rogue shark suddenly and unpredictably invades a certain beach area or stretch of shoreline and ravages one victim after another until it is killed or tires of the game. The Great White Shark, or Maneater, is believed to be the species involved in most such massacres.

The rogue shark theory was invented by the necessity to explain the Matawan Creek Massacre, the last round in a fortnight of terror along the New Jersey coast perpetrated by an 8½-foot White Shark that killed at least four persons and ravaged a fifth. The suspect shark was executed and undeniable evidence was found in its stomach in the form of odds and ends of human anatomy.

Such a shark massacre cannot be explained except as the work of a deviant monster. Were such an act to occur anywhere on the land, the powers of society would retaliate with deterrent action strong enough to eliminate the threat or at least to placate public anxiety.

PETY

Sharks are prowlers and predators. They cover broad stretches of ocean in an unending search for food. They investigate smells and sounds. They check out the objects they see in the water and test them for edibility. They nearly always decide that the human species is inedible. While sharks may follow up the smell of human blood, or the sound of fluttering feet, or even do a final visual check, they very rarely sample human flesh.

Nevertheless, sharks do attack with a Jack-the-Ripper savagery often enough to breed strong anxieties in swimmers and divers. The purpose of this chapter is to describe techniques of avoidance and defense, and to draw from them a list of safeguards that should improve every water user's security and self-reliance.

It is worth repeating that sharks usually do not attack the people they see, and that when they do, they often make a single slashing attack that is not fatal. We have seen that shark attack has four possible motives, three of which—aggression, self-defense, and mistaken identity—have nothing to do with eating people. It is also worth repeating that alert and resourceful persons have a good chance of fending off an attacking shark and making it to safety.

The list of safeguards in this chapter is drawn partly from the recorded advice of Perry Gilbert and other experts and colleagues such as H. David Baldridge, Donald Nelson, and Stewart Springer, and partly from my own analysis of the facts and opinions related in this book. While many of these safeguards are useful as general precautions, they are written specifically for use in *shark-populated waters*.

It must be left to each swimmer or diver to decide whether particular waters are, in fact, shark populated. Many clues can be drawn from this book about the places, times, and conditions under which sharks become abundant and threatening. But judgment is personal, and each person must decide for himself, just as he would calculate from available knowledge the safety of passing through certain wild lands or of visiting certain parts of a large city.

1. Swim with others. Sharks are less likely to attack one of a close group of persons than a lone swimmer or diver. And, of couse, companions can provide help in case of trouble.

2. Remain in shallow water. Avoid swimming along the edge of a channel or near a sudden dropoff from shallow to deep water. Particularly avoid the seaward edge of offshore submerged sandbars and, if there is reason to expect sharks are prowling them, shun the inner lagoons behind such bars from high to midtide.

3. All fish, whether caught by spear, line, or net, should be removed immediately from waters occupied by people and kept in a watertight container so that no blood or body juices run into the water. Swimmers or divers should leave the water if those near them cannot be constrained to follow this advice.

4. Refrain from entering or remaining in the water if you are bleeding, and leave the water quickly if you notice another person bleeding (unless your help is needed).

5. Keep yourself inconspicuous. Choose dull colors and plain fabrics and remove jewelry and other bright accessories. Try to look as little like shark prey (seal, turtle, big fish) as possible. Avoid swimming nude.

6. Refrain from swimming or diving at dusk or after dark; i.e., from two to two-and-a-half hours before sunset until the sun is well up on the next day.

7. Move easily and gracefully and avoid any thrashing or violent disturbance of the water. Particularly avoid dangling your hands and feet from a raft or paddling with jerky strokes. Leave any area where splashing and vigorous horseplay is going on.

8. If you spot a shark, scream a warning to others, then stay cool and retreat methodically but swiftly from the area to the nearest boat or beach. Swim smoothly away, keeping the shark in view unless it reaches striking range; then try to scare it off with vigorous aggressive arm waving and splashing.

9. If the shark lunges at you from close range, fight it off with the best weapon you have—knife, stick, spear, camera—and avoid hand-to-hand combat. Try to strike the shark in the eyes or gills or ram a heavy object into its mouth.

10. Learn everything you can about the water you are preparing to swim or dive into; others cannot be depended upon to warn you. Know if the waters are shark-populated under the prevailing conditions of murkiness, temperature, tide, and weather. This knowledge is necessary to enable you to employ successfully many of the safeguards listed above.

Avoiding the Risk

Place is a primary determinant. We have found that the risk of attack is much higher in one place than another. The main features of locale to consider are distance from shore, depth of the water, and configurations of the sea floor that bring deep water into the proximity of bathing areas, sandbars, or offshore reefs.

Conditions of the water are also strong factors at times. High temperatures and murky waters may increase the risk of attack in waters inhabited by sharks. The time of day is critically important, too.

The incidence of attack on swimmers is far higher at night than in the daytime. Many shark species are nocturnal and are adapted to night feeding by virtue of their acute sense of smell and ability to sonically detect and visually target moving prey in dim light. Given the generally nocturnal way of life of the dangerous sharks, it is risky to swim at night in shark-populated waters. Also, darkness makes it more difficult either to spot an approaching shark or to defend oneself against it.

There is a strong suggestion in the recorded cases that the risk of attack is higher in murky than in clear waters. Ocean murkiness, or turbidity, can arise from silt discharges of coastal rivers, from high algal growth in the water, or from wind or currents stirring up the bottom sediments. From whichever source it springs, one should avoid shark-populated waters that are murky.

Clearly the risk of attack is higher in deep water. We have found that while the average bather remains in water not deeper than wading depth, 38 percent of shark attacks on swimmers occurred in water more than 5 feet deep. It is not surprising, then, that there should also be a strong correlation between distance from shore and the probability of attack. Consequently, one should restrain the impulse to swim out over one's head in shark-populated waters and one should never go without a companion.

Both beachgoers and swimmers should keep a sharp lookout for a fin, a large shadow, and schools of small bait fish that may be followed by hunting sharks. This advice should be heeded in shallow waters as well as in deep because many shark species with the reputation for attacking man are coastal species that follow their prey into the shallows.

The risk from sharks appears highest around reefs, rocks, ridges, and other features of the sea bottom, particularly those that rise up next to channels that offer easy deep-water access for attackers. Nineteen percent of recorded attacks occurred in the vicinity of sea-bottom features such as sandbars and coral reefs where there is relatively shallow water close to channels, troughs, or other deeper waters from which the shark can sneak up on the unsuspecting victim without having to cross an expanse of shallow water.

In shark-populated waters, swimmers and divers should avoid places adjacent to channels, troughs, or dropoffs to deep water.

Sharks may also be found in the deep-water lagoons that lie inside the offshore sandbars so common to sandy beachfronts. These may be particularly risky places just before or after high tide and should be avoided in shark-populated waters.

Restraint on Activities

Many things that people do increase the hazard of attack in shark-populated waters. Specific high-risk activities include thrashing about in the water, swimming nude, paddling surfboards or rafts, provoking small sharks, or carrying dead fish through the water.

Sharks are attracted by the vigorous splashing that is typical of horseplay and erratic swimming. In shark-populated waters, it is prudent to avoid any sort of splashing, most especially after a shark has been sighted. Smooth and graceful swimming strokes are preferred. Water sports involving vigorous splashing are better conducted in pools. Flotation devices are better floated upon or towed than propelled by paddling with hands and feet because the splashing movements made by people using air mattresses, beach rafts, surfboards, and other flotation devices are

*English Channel swimmer Linda McGill swims in wire mesh cage pulled behind a boat
as she becomes the first person to cross the widest point of Port Phillip Bay,
Australia, a shark-infested, twenty-five-mile stretch of water .*

attractive to sharks. The predators may interpret the sounds as those of wounded and thrashing fish.

We have also found that sharks are highly sensitive to and attracted by certain odors in the water, particularly those of blood or other bodily fluids that suggest the presence of a meal. Sharks are able to locate wounded fish from long distances away by following the scent trails carried downdrift by currents and tides. Similarly, the presence of human blood must be considered a definite shark attractant and excitant. Sea disasters involving wounded castaways attract sharks from long distances—the blood released at these scenes incites them to strike struggling survivors or attack rafts containing bleeding victims.

The obvious conclusion is that one should re-

frain from entering shark-infested waters while bleeding. And of course, if injured while in the water, discretion requires that one leave by the most expeditious means possible. While there is no direct evidence that menstrual bleeding has ever encouraged sharks to attack, a menstruating woman should certainly be cautious about going into shark-populated waters.

People under the surface, diving and/or spear-fishing, run a much greater risk of attack. Many experts have suggested that a diver is especially vulnerable because he looks like a seal or some other typical shark fare. Other experts suggest that they stimulate shark aggression because they look like large marine creatures who are competing for the shark's food.

I have reasoned that the risk of attack may be

many times higher for submerged divers than for swimmers or waders. Therefore, one must exercise considerable caution when diving in shark-populated waters and should under no circumstances remain there after a shark has been sighted. The danger is exceptionally high when fish are being speared and are bleeding into the water.

Enough tests show sharks to be attracted to certain colors such as "yum-yum yellow." At the least, when swimming in shark-infested waters, one should minimize conspicuousness and be cautious about yellow apparel, substituting subdued colors in patterns that do not contrast sharply with the surrounding environment. For the same reason, it is inadvisable to swim unclothed when one has white bathing suit marks contrasting with a dark tan. Where a high degree of caution is required, one should leave behind reflective rings, watches, and other accessories. Black wetsuits that make one resemble a seal or other natural prey of sharks should be avoided where visibility is poor or where sharks are known to feed on such prey.

In color selection, a conflict may arise because yellow and orange-yellow facilitate visibility and enhance rescues at sea. Such colors are therefore routinely used for lifeboats, life jackets, scuba tanks, and many other items. One must calculate the risks, then, and choose a color according to whether the shark menace is greater than the risk of being lost at sea.

We have seen that lone swimmers are particularly vulnerable. This is not surprising to anyone familiar with predatory behavior because predators typically select and attack a single prey at a time —especially one that is disabled or looks different.

While most of us would quickly leave the scene on spotting a shark, there is a type of machismo that insists on remaining and tempting fate by provoking the creature. Like other animals, a shark, if threatened, cornered, or wounded, may violently turn on its molester. Even small sharks have the strength and dexterity to inflict a good deal of harm. One should never provoke a shark. Fourteen percent of all attacks on persons (a high proportion of whom were divers) were the result of deliberate provocation by the victim.

Threatening a shark may be as dangerous as spearing one. Jone Waitaiti, a 28-year-old Fijian, tried to spear a "tame" looking 7-foot shark, but missed

—the shark did not. It charged, bit off a chunk of Waitaiti's arm, and swam away. (C #1187)

Many foolish swimmers attempt to snatch small sharks out of the water by their tails with bad results. For example, on July 2, 1959, 13-year-old King Scherer tried this trick on a 2½ foot Nurse Shark at Delray Beach, Florida. The shark sank its teeth into the boy's arm and held on as Scherer swam 150 yards to the beach. There the shark was finally dislodged.

Approach and Attack

Because there is a remote chance that a shark might enter your life, it is useful to know how best to avoid serious trouble. Sharks have definite patterns of approach and there are immediate defensive moves to make.

Most sharks are seen passing in the distance. Their normal reaction is to continue placidly about their own business. However, a shark may hesitate, look you over from afar, or circle you at a good distance. The rule for such an encounter is to watch the shark carefully, scan the surrounding area for any more, and prepare your defense strategy in case the shark threatens—all this while leaving the water in a cool and rhythmic manner, rapidly but without panic. If the spearfishers gathered off the Farallon Islands on January 14, 1962, had taken such precautions and vacated the scene, Floyd Pair might not have been grievously wounded.

Pair, twenty-nine, had been spearfishing with a group of 100 other divers. Some of them had spotted a 14-foot shark earlier in the day, but as it caused no trouble, the group continued to spearfish, releasing blood and fish juices into the water. Pair was surfacing just as he was struck: "It hit me first from the right side and started shaking me like a dog plays with a bone. I spit out my mouthpiece, and yelling 'Shark! Shark!' I began jabbing at the shark's snout with my spear. He let loose of me." Pair was rescued and the other spearfishers were cleared from the water. A radio-hailed helicopter delivered the injured man from boat to hospital and his life was saved. He lost blood and chunks from his leg and buttocks, but the shark's teeth had just missed his femoral artery. (C #1001)

Floyd Pair being helped onto a stretcher as he arrives at Central Emergency Hospital in North Sacramento, California, after being mauled by a shark off the Farallon Islands.

In any attack, the first rule is to remain cool and to avoid panic. For one thing, even a large shark may be as frightened of you as you are of it. In *The Silent World,* Jacques Cousteau tells of one shark encounter in the Cape Verde Islands that confirms this:

    At a distance of forty feet there appeared from the grey haze the lead-white bulk of a twenty-five-foot *Carcharodon carcharias,* the only shark species that all specialists agree is a confirmed maneater. . . . The brute was swimming lazily. . . . Then, the shark saw us. His reaction was the last conceivable one. In pure fright, the monster voided a cloud of excrement and departed at an incredible speed.

If the shark does begin to show undue interest in you, you will most probably have time to move to safety. An aggressive shark may position itself to circle you before it strikes. Or it may assume a threat posture—a behavior pattern similar to a cat arching its back—that has been interpreted as an intimidation stance. Donald Nelson discovered this with Pacific gray reef sharks which, he observed, were swimming very curiously just prior to attack: the pectoral fins were extended down and forward 60 degrees from their normal position, the nose was tilted upward, and the back was arched. The shark then swam stiffly with almost as much head as tail motion. The stance may be followed by a high-speed lunge at the invader, but usually the shark waits for the invader to withdraw, then returns to normal swimming.

Divers who observe the shark positioning itself, circling, or posturing should retreat immediately to the safety of a boat or shallow water, or swim toward other divers. Swimmers who notice a fin, a shadow, or circling movements should seek the security of a boat or dry land. Retreat should be *orderly*. Spearfishers should leave their catches to the sharks and vacate the water. Others nearby should be warned immediately.

If the shark does approach closely before you can escape to safety, there are several ways to scare it off. You must calculate your odds carefully and decide whether counterattack is a better bet than continued retreat. Divers are often able to intimidate a shark by charging it underwater. Charging the shark was reported to have the desirable effect in 40 percent of the cases where it was tried. Swimmers can try aggressive, directed, defensive splashing to compel the shark to withdraw from the field. Once the shark is already threatening you, splashing becomes a defense rather than a provocation.

Depending on the shark's purpose, the first direct contact may be either a bump, a scrape, a raking bite, or a concerted assault. In 30 percent of attacks in the official case files, the shark first made a trial run on the victim—that is, a close pass without making contact. In other cases, the shark grazed the victim, its spiny skin and rough-edged fins causing severe cuts and abrasions, possibly for the purpose of drawing blood or body juice to sample the target for edibility, as expert H. David Baldridge suggests. After a close first pass, scrape, or bump, you may have enough time to prepare your defense or retreat. If you are grazed by a shark among a crowd of other bathers, however, the shark may be charging another victim, and you should prepare for a possible rescue.

Once you are scraped, bumped, or raked, you must assume that the shark will continue the attack, often in successive charges. Various means of aggressive defenses are now appropriate.

A "bump," if it is not a test of edibility, may mean the shark is defending its territory or that the unwary swimmer or diver has blundered onto a scene of shark courtship. Often, victims have reported only a tingling sensation or scratch. On later examination, the "scratch" often turns out to be a severe laceration caused by the raking of the skin with the shark's upper teeth. Like a "bump," such raking may be a preliminary to a full-scale attack or just a single act of aggression or test whereby the shark learns it is not further interested. A one-shot raking attack usually leaves deep slash-type lacerations.

Once the shark charges, you still have a chance. You are at a disadvantage without a weapon, but many persons have saved themselves with their bare hands. People have defended themselves actively by kicking the shark, hitting it with their hands, or digging fingers into its eyes or gills. They have defended themselves passively by riding the shark, by playing dead, or by curling into a ball to protect vulnerable arms and legs. There are probably as many ways to defend oneself as there are methods of attack, but some seem to work better than others.

When retreat is not feasible, it is probably better, even if weaponless, to attempt to fight the shark off by any means rather than do nothing. In only a few instances does counterattack appear to have worsened the situation for the victim. The best choice is to go for the eyes. Second best is the gills. Poking the shark, kicking it, or striking it have been reported as successful one-third of the time, but these methods of defense are risky in that they expose the victim's arms and legs to the jaws of the shark. On the other hand, rescuers were successful in half their attempts to aid victims by striking, kicking or poking the shark. Possession of a weapon, even a plain stick, will greatly improve the counterattack.

Rescuers of shark attack victims usually fare rather well. They are seldom attacked themselves because of the shark's single-minded nature in pursuing its first-chosen victim. A rescuer should use whatever approach suits the conditions. Most of the escape and counterattack techniques that have worked for victims under attack will work as well and often better for the rescuer. The object is to get the victim out of the water as quickly as possible. Once he is in a boat or on the beach, priority should be given to stopping profuse bleeding with tourniquet or pressure-point application and to providing shock remedies. Whenever conditions permit, and particularly when the trip to shore or boat is extended, emergency care should be performed immediately and while the victim is still in the water.

Divers and Fishermen

Divers fare better than other victims of shark attack for three reasons. First, because they are underwater, they are better able to see the attacker and respond with appropriate evasive or defensive actions. Second, divers by nature and experience are less likely to panic under attack. Third, divers frequently carry devices that are useful as weapons, particularly knives and spear guns.

Divers almost always swim in pairs or groups, a practice that not only works to deter sharks from attacking, but also provides help when rescue is required.

As we have found, most underwater shark "encounters" consist of observing a shark swimming in the distance. A good first reaction in such an instance is to freeze and remain motionless until the shark has passed from view, hopefully without noticing you. In 1941, and for many years previously, this practice was followed by divers of the Torres Strait on the coast of northern Australia, who dove to depths of 60 feet or more for pearls. According to a medical officer stationed at the hospital on Thursday Island, as quoted by shark expert G. P. Whitley in *The Fishes of Australia:*

" . . . a diver rarely fails to see at least one shark during any day. They consider that they have nothing to fear from sharks less than six feet in length and are of opinion that a strong swimmer is more than a match for such sharks. . . . The divers have found that a shark is more likely to attack a moving object than a stationary one, and, if a large shark is seen, they keep perfectly still by holding on to the edge of a reef on the bottom of the sea. They believe that if they move about or swim away the chances of an attack are considerable. On the surface, they also keep perfectly still while waiting to be picked up. . . . "

Perhaps the most remarkable passive defense was put up by abalone hunter Frank Logan near Tomales Point, California, on July 27, 1968. The water was cold, murky, and a gathering spot for seals, a favorite food of the Great White Shark. Logan, in a black wetsuit, was swimming through the kelp near a dropoff. Without warning, an 18-foot Great White seized his torso from shoulder to waist in its massive jaws, and began to carry him through the water. Believing that if the shark shook him he would be torn apart, Logan went limp and "played dead." Then, remarkably, the shark appears to have snapped off Logan's heavy weight belt which fell into its throat. In order to disgorge the belt, the shark had to release the diver. When he did, Logan dashed for the safety of his boat. Two hundred stitches were required to close his wounds, but he considers himself lucky to have escaped with his life. (C #1569)

Divers with scuba tanks have the advantage of time, as noted by my colleague Richard B. Stone of the National Marine Fisheries Service, designer of "artificial reefs," structures made of old car bodies and worn-out tires that attract multitudes of fish, along with boat fishermen and spearfishers. Stone told me about two scuba-equipped spearfishers who were spearing fish on a reef off Charleston, South Carolina, and were carrying the catch on stringers tied to their belts. Suddenly a large shark appeared on the scene and charged one of the men. Luckily he was able to jump into the front seat of a Chevrolet, close the left door and roll up the window. Frustrated, the shark took off after his buddy, who had streaked for the boat just in time to haul himself in. The shark then returned to the Chevrolet to try again for the first diver, but he had exited out the right door of the car and fled for the boat. The shark wheeled and raced after him. But again, the shark reached the boat just as his target left the water.

A diver who sees a shark charging can try to intimidate the attacker on the theory that while fleeing will encourage pursuit, moving aggressively toward it will cause retreat. This kind of aggressive defense has a long history, going back to Pliny (23–79 A.D.) who wrote, "The only way to deal with this [attack] is to go straight for them and frighten them, since they fear man no less than he fears them."

Modern shark expert Don Nelson believes that divers can intimidate sharks by shouting at them and by using the arms in vigorous threatening gestures. The idea is to appear as little like a helpless prey as possible, to make yourself larger by extending your arms, and to behave more like a predator than a victim. The best time for such a countercharge is when the shark is from 10 to 15 feet away, close enough to see and appreciate the implied threat. One must consider such bravado only a *substitute* for retreat; it is perhaps more to be relied on by experienced divers and students of shark behavior. In any event, it is worth trying if it doesn't interfere with one's subsequent physical defense against the shark.

When a shark refuses to be scared off, the defense must be escalated. With a spear gun or billy, one can often fend off the attacker by pushing against its nose and riding over or under its body as it lunges past. This should deflect the charge because, steering mainly from their tail with some help from their pectoral fins, sharks cannot maneuver well in close quarters. But remember, Hammerheads cannot be so successfully fended off in this manner because they steer with the hammer, the planing device attached to their heads just above the jaws.

If the shark has managed to grab you, jab at its eyes or gills with whatever weapon is handy—a spear gun, knife, or billy. Avoid contact with the shark's bare skin, however, for its sandpaper hide may scrape you raw, and blood in the water will only further excite the creature. Proof that a successful defense can be put up even if the shark hits without warning was given by Rolf Ericson.

On April 16, 1961, near Biscayne Bay, Florida, this spearfisher was chasing an erratically swimming grouper that had been recently wounded. As Ericson moved in to spear it, his legs were seized from behind by a 10-foot Tiger Shark which may have been pursuing the same grouper. Ericson struck the shark's snout hard, and it released its hold. Circling, the shark came at him again, but the diver fended it off with his spear gun. This second maneuver gained him the time to reach the safety of his boat. (C #928)

Divers attacked by sharks have defended themselves in a number of remarkable ways. Off New South Wales, Australia, on April 15, 1968, Rodney Castle resorted to an unusual defense when his hand was swallowed by a 6-foot Bronze Whaler shark. Realizing he could lose a finger or his whole hand if he attempted to wrench it free, Castle threw his other arm around the beast and went "shark-back riding" for a distance of some 30 yards with his hand clamped firmly in its mouth. Finally the shark opened its jaws, apparently trying for a better grip. Castle quickly yanked his bleeding hand away, dismounted, and fled. The attacker swam off. (C #1456)

Of the weapons employed by victims in the official cases, knives seemed the most effective, with a success rate of 69 percent in driving off sharks. Spears repelled sharks in 41 percent of attempts, but intensified the attacks in another 10 percent.

The shark billy, a short club that divers use to poke approaching sharks, has been successful in deflecting the attackers in 53 percent of reported attempts. But, most of the successful defenses with billies are probably not reported, and therefore the statistics give too little credit to the shark billy.

The bang stick or powerhead is a most effective weapon. It is loaded with a shotgun shell on the end of a short shaft that fires on impact. When driven against a shark, preferably in such a vulnerable spot as on top of the head between the eyes, the bang stick is nearly 100 percent effective. However, it is a lethal weapon in the hands of a careless or inexperienced diver or malefactor, and has been banned in some parts of the world. Because the noise and the ensuing thrashing and blood may draw other sharks to the vicinity, one must leave the water immediately after firing the bang stick. The danger of doing otherwise was demonstrated by John Harding, 25, an underwater photographer. On a Friday the 13th in November 1964, Harding was shooting pictures near North Solitary Island, Australia. Two Sand Tiger Sharks (called Grey Nurse locally) were scaring the subject fish away, so he killed one with a bang stick. Going after the second, he was suddenly confronted by an attacking nine-foot White Shark. As the fish hurtled toward him, Harding destroyed it by holding his weapon straight ahead and letting the shark hit it, head on.

The diver's best defense, however, is avoidance of the stimuli that trigger shark attack. Those stimuli that signal the diver's presence or suggest the diver as prey are odors of blood or body fluids, struggling and splashing sounds, and visual resemblance to shark foe or food.

Carrying speared fish around or remaining in

waters where fish have been speared and are discharging blood and body fluids is hazardous. Speared fish should be taken directly to a watertight container or boat. If threatened by a shark on the way, the catch should be released. It certainly makes better sense to give up your catch than to sacrifice an arm or leg.

It is obvious that a diver who has been cut or scraped and is bleeding should neither enter the water nor remain in the water. Also some ingenuity could well be exercised in arranging the wetsuit and gear to look as little like a seal, turtle, large fish or other natural prey as possible.

All manner of small watercraft are subject to attack. Sharks have nuzzled, bumped, bashed, or bitten a variety of rafts, canoes, launches, and boats. The crafts most frequently attacked are fishing boats, which attract sharks by discharging fish blood and body fluids into the sea.

Veteran shark fisherman Wilson Wright of Sanibel Island, Florida, reported to me the following typical incident: "I was out with my friend Herbert Heller in a small 12-foot skiff—a Sears Roebuck "Kingfisher"—one February morning in 1974. We were fishing near the Sanibel Beach at a place called the Rocks and catching some pretty nice trout. We had taken a half a dozen by 10:00 A.M. and had them stringered and hung overside. I had just suggested that we might become shark bait with those bleeding fish in the water, when Herb sang out: 'Fin! A big one!' Seconds later he was almost knocked out of the boat when a 9-foot Bull Shark hit us hard enough to put a large permanent dent in that plastic hull. He didn't bite; he just rammed it with his nose. I don't mind sharks nuzzling the boat, they do that all the time. But bashing into it like that is darn scary." The obvious way to prevent attack is to keep the fish in a watertight container, either in the water or in the boat.

Protecting the Public

As shark protection expert Perry Gilbert explained to me, "There are three hot spots in the world for sharks: the coasts around Durban, South Africa, and Sydney, Australia, and the whole Florida Peninsula. Both South Africa and Australia have set up effective countermeasures to protect the public." What Dr. Gilbert did not have to tell me is that Florida does nothing to protect either tourists or residents. The reason for this is clear —the tourist industry of the state would rather take its chances on losing a few bathers each year (at least twelve are attacked during the average year in Florida according to Dr. Gilbert) than to undertake a concerted protection program that would considerably reduce attacks but would bring the shark danger out in the open and perhaps discourage a fraction of tourists from coming to Florida.

With no less cause for concern about their tourist revenues, South African and Australian communities have created special shark meshing nets that are set and patrolled during the high-hazard season. There are also shark watchtowers at those beaches where the layout of the ocean floor does not permit nets.

In South Africa, meshing is done with a double system of nets, set parallel to the beach outside the breakers, along a path sharks are likely to cross as they approach swimming areas. The nets are patrolled by a special boat once or twice a week; dead sharks are removed and live ones killed and towed out to sea. From 1952 to 1962, no attacks took place at Durban, although in the previous twelve years, twenty-one attacks had occurred in the same area. Enough sharks are killed to reduce their populations, as shown by the rate of decline of catches. In 1952, in the nets set up at Durban, 552 were caught. By 1962, the number was 107.

Meshing is practical off beaches that gradually shelve into the sea. But in areas with many rocks or sharp dropoffs, or where the coast extends in an unbroken line with no harbor facilities for a patrol boat, other means must be employed.

In Australia, lookouts man mobile scaffold towers on certain beaches. Stationed high above the water, the shark-watcher can observe a large shark approaching in time to warn people out of the water. In peak danger periods, helicopters are added to the watch. While shark-watching is feasible when the water is clear, it is not so useful when the water is murky.

Another excellent measure in protecting coastal areas is banning the discharge of garbage and other organic matter such as slaughterhouse or fishhouse wastes into the water. These wastes release odors and set up an olfactory field that attracts sharks from many miles away. In the official cases analyzed for this factor, garbage or other organic wastes were present in the area of the shark incident, and thus associated with attack, in one out of four cases.

In view of the horrifying consequences of shark attack and the cost in human life and suffering, it is surprising that U.S. beach communities do not overcome the commercial motive and take advantage of all means at their disposal to minimize the possibility of shark attack. A case in point is Daytona Beach, Florida, where the hazard of shark attack accelerates with the May–June shark-spawning season and remains for the summer.

The first publicized attack of the 1975 season came in early June when Edward Bassett, a seventeen-year-old high school student, was struck while lolling on his surfboard in waist-deep water off Daytona. The shark hit from behind, knocking the boy off the board and mangling his right foot. Kicking the shark's head with his other foot, Bassett tore himself free of the jaws and saved himself by racing for the beach.

Neither Bassett nor any other bather had been warned, although one city commissioner called the 1975 shark infestation the worst in his experience. Five days previously, in the same area, a ten-year-old girl had been badly mauled by a shark and the incident was crassly covered up—no story appeared in the local paper.

By August, three more bathers had been struck along the Daytona coast, raising the seasonal total to five reported victims. The fifth and worst of these tragedies occurred just off Daytona Beach near the Zelda Boulevard approach. Henry Peterson, a twenty-year-old student, was vacationing with his parents at the Daytona Campground, spending as much time as he could at the beach. On August 12, he was drifting along about 60 feet from the beach, draped over a small orange raft, when suddenly a large shark hit hard from the rear, knocking him into the waist-deep water and tearing chunks of flesh from his right calf. Peterson's screams brought Julius Anthony to the scene so quickly that he was able to fight off the shark on its second attack and to help Peterson scramble aboard the raft.

Lifeguard Captain Bob Wheeler credits Anthony with saving Peterson's life. In addition, Charles Peterson, the boy's father, told me, "Henry was aware, having read *Jaws* [a popular novel about shark attack], and knew immediately what had happened and what he had to do to save himself." At the hospital there seemed hope that Peterson's leg could be saved. Surgeons struggled from Tuesday until Saturday morning before they gave up and removed the mangled leg just below the knee.

Charles Peterson, still shocked by the tragedy, was unable to understand why the city gave no warning and provided no protection. Furthermore, he stated, "They still refuse to clean up the fishing pier at the beach, which is a major source of attraction to sharks. Fish are cleaned here and the guts thrown into the water along with discarded bait and other matter that is food for sharks."

Thomas Sweeney, a local pilot, emphatically believes that something more needs to be done than simply cleaning up the pier. "There are sharks all up and down this coast," he told me. "I've seen as many as twenty-seven large ones mixed in with the bathers on one pass over the Daytona beaches." In 1974, Sweeney performed a six-week demonstration shark watch at Daytona in conjunction with his regular advertising flights during which he tows signs promoting various products and services. He radioed precise shark locations directly to the lifeguard towers, and mobile loudspeaker units were dispatched directly to the scene to clear the water of bathers.

But Sweeney's shark patrol was too much for the city fathers. When the 1974 demonstration ended and Sweeney proposed an annual budget of $2,500 for a three-plane continuous watch during each year's shark season, they vetoed it on budgetary grounds, although $2,500 seems a trivial amount for 1,300 flying hours of surveillance. While attack after attack occurred during the 1975 summer season, the city fathers stood firm against alarming the tourists. The local newspapers gradually dropped their support of Sweeney's plan, announcing that Daytona's problem was no worse than that of any other beach.

Then came the mutilation of Henry Peterson and the leg amputation of August 16. On August 18–19, the City Commissioners met once more to reconsider matters. As concern mounted, a committee was appointed to deal with the issue.

To one unfamiliar with the commercial system of the United States, it must be difficult to understand why tourist communities refuse to protect the public from sharks. But in a freewheeling free-enterprise economy, any constraints imposed upon customers in one community will shift the competitive advantage to a neighboring community. The only solution, then, for Daytona would be to encourage the assignment of shark protection responsibility to the state government so that uniform safeguards can be applied to Florida.

On the other side of Florida, the west coast, there is a different environmental situation and a different set of attitudes. Susan Siltanen, a long-time resident of the Tampa region, told me, "Over here we chalk up the attacks to the Yankees' lack of respect for the sea and its dangers. I don't remember a summer from 1962 to 1970 when I was working on the beach at Santa Maria Island that we didn't have at least one attack on a swimmer. These northerners come down, ignore the no-swimming signs put up for shark protection, and plunge into the water by the south channel where the fishing pier is. They do it at dusk or at night, and sure they get hit. They're just asking for it. But still, maybe we should try harder to protect them against their own stupidity. Like, for instance, maybe those no-swimming signs should say something about sharks."

Susan is right—people do have to be educated, warned, and protected by the community from dangers they have not experienced and know too little about. They must be warned about these strangers of the sea so they will be respectful of their powers and wary of their actions.

READING LIST

Baldridge, H. David, *Shark Attack,* New York: Berkley Publishing Corp., New York, 1974.

———, "Shark Attack: A Program of Data Reduction and Analysis," in *Contributions from the Mote Marine Laboratory,* Vol. 1, No. 2, Sarasota, Fla., 1974.

Budker, Paul, *The Life of Sharks,* New York: Columbia University Press, 1971.

Butler, Jean Campbell, *Danger Shark!,* Boston: Little, Brown & Co., 1964.

Casey, John G., *Anglers' Guide to Sharks of the Northeastern United States,* Bureau of Sport Fisheries and Wildlife Circular No. 179, Washington, D.C.: U.S. Government Printing Office, April, 1964.

Clark, Eugenie, *The Lady and the Sharks,* New York: Harper & Row, Publishers, 1969.

Coppelson, V. M., *Shark Attack,* Sydney, Australia: Angus & Robertson, 1962.

Davies, David H., *About Sharks and Shark Attack,* Pietermaritzburg, South Africa: Shuter and Shooter, 1964.

Gilbert, P. W., ed., *Sharks and Survival,* Boston: D. C. Heath, 1963.

Halstead, Bruce W., *Dangerous Marine Animals,* Cambridge, Md.: Cornell Maritime Press, 1959.

Lineaweaver, Thomas H., and Backus, Richard H., *The Natural History of Sharks,* Philadelphia: J. B. Lippincott Co., 1970.

Mundus, Capt. Frank, and Wisner, William, *Sportfishing for Sharks,* New York: The Macmillan Co., 1971.

Norman, J. R., and Fraser, F. C., *Giant Fishes, Whales and Dolphins,* New York: W. W. Norton & Co., Inc., 1938.

Sosin, Mark, and Clark, John, *Through the Fish's Eye,* New York: Harper & Row, 1973.

Whitley, G. P., *The Fishes of Australia, Part I: Sharks,* Sydney, Australia: Royal Zoological Society of New South Wales, 1940.

PHOTO CREDITS

The publishers are grateful to the following for permission to use the photographs in this book: Ron Church/Photo Researchers, p. 49 (bottom); Bruce Coleman, Inc., p. 43; Ben Cropp, p. 34, p. 39, p. 53; Robert L. Dunne/Bruce Coleman, Inc., p. 20; Andrew A. Gifford/National Audubon Society, p. 44 (top left); Globe Photos, p. 26, p. 44 (bottom left); I. A. Halevik (Courtesy National Marine Fisheries Service), p. 16 (bottom); Peter Lake/Photo Researchers, pp. 8–9; Marineland of Florida, p. 28, p. 33, p. 47, p. 48, p. 49 (top); Tom McHugh/Photo Researchers, p. 40; National Audubon Society, p. 34 (lower right), p. 36 (upper right), p. 108; National Game Fish Association, p. 36 (lower left); R. R. Pawlowski/Bruce Coleman, Inc., p. 50; Pictures Incorporated, p. 46; Roy Pincy/Globe Photos, p. 44 (right); Scott Ransom, p. 35, p. 94; Scott Ransom/Photo Researchers, p. 36 (upper left); Flip Schulke/Black Star, p. 21 (top), p. 25, p. 30; Peter Stockpole/Time Inc., p. 10, p. 17, p. 21 (bottom); Valerie Taylor, p. 6, p. 73; United Press International, p. 12. p. 15, p. 16 (top), p. 18, p. 22. p. 23, p. 32, p. 37, p. 38, p. 51, p. 58. p. 60, p. 72, p. 97, p. 99, p. 107; Harold Wes Pratt (Courtesy National Marine Fisheries Service), p. 24 (both), p. 55.

INDEX